Elizabeth Street Café

Breakfast   Lunch   Dinner   Sweets

ELIZABETH

STREET

CAFE

Tom
Moorman

Larry
McGuire

with
Julia Turshen

Skagen - Brakhage

Capitol
OF TEXAS

Roadhouse
RELICS
VISIT OUR GALLERY
featuring
VINTAGE NEON
SIGNS & DECOR
FOR HOMES
RESTAURANTS
& MOVIE SETS
(512) 442-NEON

Tom's Introduction

Elizabeth Street Café (ESC, as many like to call it), which we opened in December 2012, is located in south-central Austin, Texas, at the corner of South First and Elizabeth Streets. When I moved to Austin in 2003, it was a very different town than it is now. South First Street was a jumble of used car dealerships, inexpensive Mexican joints, and repair shops.

I first lived in Clarksville, on the north side of the Colorado River close to downtown, in a barely inhabitable blue bungalow with my then-girlfriend-now-wife, Lauren, and my good buddy Caleb (who contributed a huge watercolor of George of the Jungle that now hangs in ESC's main dining room). I found a job as a sous-chef on the opening team of a sushi restaurant on Sixth Street, which also made Japanese fusion food. The consulting chef was a colorful Canadian guy from Toronto. Together, we quickly discovered all the Asian markets, Chinese restaurants, and late-night karaoke bars that Austin had to offer.

I've always loved Asian flavors: Before I moved to Austin, I had lived and worked in Montreal (at Toqué and later at Globe under the guys who now run Joe Beef) and also in New York (at Mesa Grill). I fondly recall lots of late-night dinners after long shifts: in both of the cities' Chinatowns, Thai noodle spots, Korean barbecue restaurants, and dim sum joints on those rare Sundays when I didn't have to work. Austin didn't offer quite the variety that both Montreal and New York had, but we tried everything available, especially on the north side of town, where the majority of the Austin's Asian population resides.

Shortly after arriving in Austin, I met my business partner, Larry McGuire, through some friends from my hometown of San Antonio. Larry took me to Tam Deli, a cafe he had been going to since high school, run by Tam Bui and Tran Ngoc, sisters who came to America during the Vietnam War and then put themselves through business school at the University of Texas. Much of what I think of as proper Vietnamese cooking we learned while eating there. Having spent most of my adult life on the East Coast, in Central America, and in Europe, I had eaten plenty of Chinese and Japanese food and a decent amount of Thai food in Montreal. While I knew my way around a bottle of fish sauce and rice noodles, my real introduction to Vietnamese food happened at Tam Deli. The first time I tried a bowl of their *pho*, fresh *bún* salad, and *bánh mì* on their perfect bread, I was amazed and incredibly inspired. I became a devoted customer and student, dedicating all of my free time to studying Vietnamese cooking.

The initial menu for Elizabeth Street Café was not the only Asian menu I had jotted down in the hope that it would someday materialize into a restaurant (the first was a heavily Szechuan-influenced Chinese and dim sum menu in 2006). But when the space on South First presented itself, Larry and I thought it would be perfect for a Vietnamese cafe.

Today we love that ESC a place to go to anytime. It is great for breakfast meetings, quick lunches, and lingering dinners in which plate after plate promises something bright and memorable. Our range is wide: we've got everything from as assortment of homemade macarons (page 152) to spicy Singapore Noodles with Gulf Shrimp and Roasted Pork (page 102) and Bún Bo Hue (page 38), which will cure even the worst of colds. We like to think we have something for everyone, a place where a grandmother can take her grandkid and they can both find something they love. It's a favorite among neighborhood locals, people across town, tourists, and celebrities alike. It's the place I want to go to every day.

While I was living in Clarksville, I didn't often make it to south of the river (the neighborhood where Elizabeth Street Café now is). I would occasionally have lunch at Guero's Taco Bar or dinner at Vespaio for a solid lasagna. When friends started moving in that direction though, I followed suit. The South Congress area had just started to expand. I moved into a little house on Eva Street, one block west of Congress, directly behind a car dealership where our restaurant Perla's now sits.

I drove down South First Street every morning to work at our first restaurant, Lamberts Downtown Barbecue, and I drove back on it every night. Other than that drive and the margaritas at Polvos, I didn't think much about the street. Bouldin Creek Café, a vegetarian and vegan restaurant, was the only other busy spot on the street. It was a gathering place for Austin's self-proclaimed freaks and hippies. I met an architect there for coffee one morning and remember thinking how strange it was, but I liked it. I returned many times after. The property had several huge heritage oaks and a beautiful mimosa tree, all of which gave it an almost tropical feel.

Bouldin Creek Café was an old box of a building, with a lean-to on one side and a rickety screened-in porch in the back. Behind it by the creek was a cute bungalow in various states of disrepair. The main building used to be covered in murals and you can still see remnants of them around the bottom of our foundation.

Our original plan was to do a light remodel but keep the funky, divey vibe. We soon discovered that the building had to be pretty much scrapped. The permit required us to keep two walls, so we built on the existing floor plan. The current flow of the restaurant is actually pretty close to that of the original cafe. Since we were essentially starting from scratch, we designed an expansive kitchen with a bakery space for making our *bánh mì* bread (page 166). When we first opened, people would ask why the kitchen was so large for such a tiny restaurant. Now that we're so busy, we wish it were even bigger.

For design inspiration we looked to the French colonial architecture of Hanoi and its old cafes, like the Green Tangerine. We put in big divided windows, aqua green shutters, striped awnings, and a T-shirt Pink (literally the name of the paint color we used) door against gray stucco. The interior is a fun mash-up of old-school French and kitschy chinoiserie.

One of the things we love about Vietnamese food is how a small group of ingredients can create so many dishes, flavors, and textures. You can make something totally new by varying the width of rice noodles, using one herb over a combination, cutting a cucumber a different way, or mixing fish sauce with vinegar instead of lime juice. Vietnamese food is great anywhere, but works especially well with Texas climate. A big bowl of *pho* is just the thing on a cold, rainy day; bun and spring rolls are satisfying but light when it's hot out; and cold iceberg lettuce around a hot crêpe with plenty of mint is refreshing no matter the weather.

Like the original idea for the building, the menu started out with mostly traditional Vietnamese dishes. As the space evolved into something more thoughtful, so did the menu. We added breakfast and kids' menus, and our coffee offerings expanded. Our staple *bánh mì* bread eventually morphed into a French bread and pastry program. No one in town was doing a proper croissant or macaron, and we filled the void. We moved our long-time pastry chef, Alex Manley, from our restaurant, Perla's, to get the pastry and bread-baking kitchen started. Alex worked at bakeries in France and San Francisco, and while in Corseul, France, learned to make traditional *kouign-amann*—the traditional pastry of Brittany—which is a small cake made of laminated dough like a croissant, but coated with caramelized sugar. Alex and our other pastry chef, Jen Tucker, did an amazing job executing an ambitious program.

While writing the menu, I tested the recipes at home, spent hours at Asian markets buying different rice noodles and rice papers, sauces, pastes, and vinegars. It was scary opening a Vietnamese spot when I was just an enthusiastic fan of the food, not a bona fide Vietnamese chef. There was a lot of trial and error. In the months before opening ESC, dinners at home consisted mostly of Vietnamese dishes, with many a taco run after a failed cooking attempt. Bánh Cuôn with Twice-Cooked Pork and Herb Salad (page 106) and Crispy Pork and Shrimp Crêpe with Bean Sprouts (page 120) were especially challenging. I like to think now that all this work was great preparation for making this book.

The menu changed a lot in the early months after opening. A handful of items met some resistance from our patrons. We were stubborn with a few—like the *bánh cuôn*, which hardly sold, but we kept it on the menu because we loved it so much. Soon we got others to love it, too, and today it flies out of the kitchen.

Some dishes that we used to run as specials became so popular that we made them permanent members of the menu. The Escargots with Thai Basil–Curry Butter (page 98), Akaushi Carpaccio with Seared Shishito Peppers and Marinated Mushrooms (page 92), and Drunken Noodles with Chicken Sausage and Peanuts (page 115) are all on this list. We faced some criticism early on for lacking authenticity, but it was never our goal to be authentic. We just wanted to make food we loved with hopes that others would be happy eating it.

On the pages that follow, you'll find not only all the recipes from Elizabeth Street Café but also an extensive section on Vietnamese ingredients and equipment so that you can easily recreate the dishes in your own kitchen. If you've been to Elizabeth Street Café, we hope this book feels like a scrapbook full of memories of the meals you've enjoyed and can now revisit at home. If you've never been, consider this cookbook an open door to everything we offer, everything we've built, and everything we love—and we hope to see you there someday.

Larry's Introduction

I was born and raised in Austin, Texas, and grew up mostly in Travis Heights, the funky, hilly neighborhood just south of downtown and east of Bouldin Creek, where Elizabeth Street Café (ESC) is located. When I was sixteen, I started working for a well-known local chef named Lou Lambert at his deli and catering company, located on the just-starting-to-gentrify strip known as South Congress. Working for Lou and growing up professionally around his sister, Liz Lambert, the celebrated hotelier, encouraged me to pursue cooking and creating restaurants.

Lou helped open so many doors for me, including the literal one at 1501 South First Street where Tom and I took over the space and turned it into Elizabeth Street Café. It all happened through a phone call from Leslie More, a local caterer for whom Lou once worked. He offered us the lease for his ramshackle assortment of buildings at 1501, and that was that. At this moment, we have seven restaurants in Austin and they've all started in this kind of way (being in the right place at the right time, knowing the right locals, and having lots of good luck). This process is much like how "old Austin" worked and is the vibe that continues to live on in locally owned businesses like Elizabeth Street Café.

In addition to the well-timed lease, ESC was born out of a neighborhood desire. Tom and I had both grown tired of driving way up north to eat at our favorite Asian places and we were both craving really good coffee and a great bakery in our area. Doing Vietnamese food satisfied all our wants because the onetime French colony is a true fusion of Eastern cooking and Western baking. We were really excited to try our hand at both and wanted to use the caliber of ingredients we had grown accustomed to in fine dining, but without the trappings of high-end food. We were stoked to do a really fun and casual restaurant that blended the energy of a neighborhood bistro with the colors of colonial Hanoi.

Since we couldn't afford to travel extensively in Vietnam before we opened ESC, we did the next best thing and spent time in America's cities with thriving Vietnamese populations. We started in Houston's Little Saigon and East New Orleans, which are home to thousands of Vietnamese-owned businesses, because of to an Influx of Vietnamese refugees after the Vietnam War. (After people affiliated with the South Vietnamese government arrived, the communities grew when the expanding economy, warm climate, and proximity to the Gulf of Mexico and its shrimping [prawning] and fishing industries drew more Vietnamese blue-collar workers.) We also went to California and ate our way through Los Angeles and San Francisco (especially at Charles Phan's restaurant, the Slanted Door, which is an institution) and spent some time in New York City, looking for inspiration.

When we got back to Austin, Tom bought all the cookbooks he could find and started experimenting in his home kitchen while I worked on the business plan and design of the restaurant. We always start our concepts with a menu and Tom wrote a first draft during an airplane flight. The dishes at first leaned a bit more toward China and Thailand, but it laid the groundwork for what would ultimately become ESC's menu. Stalwarts from that first draft are still popular today, like the Singapore Noodles with Gulf Shrimp and Roasted Pork (page 102) and the Classic Tam Deli Wonton Soup (page 78). We soon incorporated Vietnamese classics like *bánh mì*, a variety of *pho*, and *bún*, all of which have become the core of our business. Our bakers came up with all kinds of inventive tropical-flavored macarons for our pastry case. After being open for only two weeks, we added breakfast and our first kids' menu to satisfy young families in the area.

Like all our projects, ESC is an ongoing huge collaboration between our talented team and our usual suspects: graphic designers, art dealers, construction guys, our neon sign dude, music programmer, landscapers, clothing designers, and more. Combined, they all create the deep layers of detail that we strive for.

Not only has the restaurant become a neighborhood fixture, it's also been a true success (we were able to pay back our sixteen local investors in just three years). For me, what is most satisfying is seeing all the ways the restaurant is used. ESC is a great spot for a quiet weekday breakfast or a rowdy weekend brunch. We see people come straight from the airport with their luggage for their *pho* fix, and we have a regular group of dads who sit at the bar for a beer while waiting for their family's Sunday take-out orders.

Tom and I have gone on to open more restaurants in our dumb-luck fashion, with him focused on food and kitchen operations and me on concept and design, but we constantly cross over into each other's realms. I still love to cook and he also has a great sense for the bottom line and a love for art and design. We continue to tinker with ESC and all our older restaurants, in the hope they will be considered institutions like the ones that have made Austin such a great place to grow up—and continue to make it one of the best cities to live in.

BREAKFAST

Sticky Rice with Ginger Sausage, Herb Salad, and Poached Eggs

FOR THE RICE:

1½ cups (330 g) Thai sticky rice (or any sweet, glutinous rice), rinsed well

Large pinch of kosher (coarse) salt

FOR THE GINGER SAUSAGE:

1 lb (455 g) ground pork (the coarser the better)

2 teaspoons kosher (coarse) salt

2 teaspoons packed dark brown sugar

½ teaspoon black pepper

1 teaspoon dried red chile flakes

1 scallion (spring onion), ends trimmed, minced

1 tablespoon minced fresh ginger

1 garlic clove, minced

½ teaspoon fish sauce

Canola (rapeseed) or vegetable oil, as needed

TO SERVE:

½ Fresno or other fresh red chile, stemmed and thinly sliced, or more to taste

2 large handfuls mixed soft herb leaves (we use mint, cilantro [coriander], and Thai basil)

2 small radishes, thinly sliced

1 teaspoon extra-virgin olive oil, plus extra for drizzling

1 teaspoon fresh lime juice

Kosher (coarse) salt

1 tablespoon unseasoned rice vinegar

4 eggs

2 tablespoons hoisin sauce

2 tablespoons sriracha

Fleur de sel

Our top-selling breakfast dish, this rice-and-eggs plate falls under the eggs Benedict umbrella on the breakfast menu. We use a generous amount of warm sticky rice as our base and serve it with our house-made breakfast sausage spiked with lots of fresh ginger, which tastes even better if you mix it a few hours—or even a day—before. We've tried cooking sticky rice many different ways and came up with a foolproof technique using a steamer and a shallow bowl. You don't need to measure the rice or the water—just set up your steaming rig properly and the rice comes out perfectly each time.

MAKE THE RICE:

Set up a conventional steamer or a bamboo steamer inside of a large pot and fill the pot with water accordingly. Bring the water to a boil. Put the rice into a dish that fits comfortably inside of the steamer and make sure the dish is large enough so that the rice comes only about ¼ inch (6 mm) up the dish. Sprinkle the rice with the salt and pour enough cool water into the dish just to cover the rice by ½ inch (1 cm). Put the dish of rice and water into the steamer, cover the steamer, and cook until the rice is tender, 20 to 25 minutes (start checking at 20 minutes). Once cooked, the rice can sit comfortably in the steamer for up to 20 minutes.

MAKE THE GINGER SAUSAGE:

Preheat the oven to 275°F (140°C/Gas Mark 1).

In a large bowl, combine the ground pork, salt, brown sugar, pepper, chile flakes, scallion, ginger, garlic, and fish sauce. Use your hands to thoroughly combine the sausage ingredients. Evenly divide the mixture into 8 patties. Place a large skillet over medium-high heat and add enough canola oil to lightly coat the surface. Cook the patties, in batches as necessary, adding more oil as needed, until browned on both sides, 2 to 3 minutes on each side. Transfer the sausage patties to a sheet pan and keep them warm in the oven while you prepare the herb salad and eggs.

TO SERVE:

In a medium bowl, combine the sliced chile, herbs, and radishes. Drizzle with 1 teaspoon olive oil and the lime juice and season to taste with salt. Reserve the mixture.

Bring a large wide saucepan of salted water to a boil, then reduce the heat to low and stir in the vinegar. Crack 1 egg into a small bowl. Stir the water gently to create a whirlpool and, while gently stirring, carefully slip the egg into the simmering water. Repeat the process as quickly as possible with the remaining eggs and work in batches as necessary, as determined by the size of your pan so that the eggs stay separate. Poach the eggs until they're barely firm to the touch, about 3 minutes. Remove the eggs with a slotted spoon and blot dry on paper towels.

Divide the rice among 4 bowls. Evenly drizzle the hoisin and the sriracha over the rice and place a poached egg on top of the rice in each of the bowls. Drizzle each poached egg with a bit of olive oil and sprinkle each egg with a pinch of fleur de sel. Place 2 sausage patties to the side of each egg and the herb salad on the other side of each egg. Serve immediately.

Crispy Vermicelli Cakes
with the Works

SERVES 4

1 Fresno or other fresh red chile, stemmed
   and thinly sliced
2 large handfuls mixed soft herb leaves
   (we use mint, cilantro [coriander], and
   Thai basil)
6 large radishes, thinly sliced
2 teaspoons extra-virgin olive oil
2 teaspoons fresh lime juice
Kosher (coarse) salt
8 oz (230 g) rice vermicelli
3 egg yolks (reserve the whites for another
   use, such as the *bánh mì* on page 32)
2 scallions (spring onions), ends trimmed,
   thinly sliced
3 tablespoons nonglutinous white rice flour
¼ cup (60 g) Clarified Butter (page 212)
1 recipe Red Roasted Pork Belly (page 218),
   sliced ¼ inch (.5 cm) thick
8 eggs, cooked to your liking
Sambal oelek chile paste, for serving

Our ode to a classic American breakfast, this is our Vietnamese spin on eggs, crispy bacon (streaky), and hash browns. We found that by combining the soaked rice noodles we use for Singapore Noodles with Gulf Shrimp and Roasted Pork (page 102) and the boiled rice noodles we always have lots of for *bún*, we could make the most delicious noodle cakes with crispy exteriors and soft, yielding interiors.

In a medium bowl, combine the sliced chile, herbs, and radishes. Drizzle with the oil and lime juice and season to taste with salt. Reserve the mixture.

Bring a medium pot of water to a boil and half of the rice noodles (4 oz/115 g) for exactly 4 minutes, stirring gently while they cook to separate them. Drain the noodles in a colander and rinse with cool water to wash off the extra starch. Let the noodles sit for 15 minutes so the excess water drains and the noodles come to room temperature—they should be a little sticky.

Meanwhile, place the remaining rice noodles (4 oz/115 g) in a large bowl of hot tap water and let them soak until they're softened, about 5 minutes. Drain, but don't rinse them.

Place all the rice noodles in a large bowl and use a pair of scissors to roughly chop them. Add the egg yolks, scallions, flour, and 2 teaspoons salt to the noodles and stir to combine. Your hands are the best tools for this, albeit messy, job.

Line a plate with paper towels and set aside. Place a large nonstick skillet over high heat and add enough clarified butter to lightly coat the surface. Divide the noodles evenly into 8 small pancake-size portions (if you have a 3-inch/8 cm ring mold, feel free to use it to make more perfect cakes) and then transfer 4 portions to the skillet. Cook the noodle cakes, pressing them down gently with a silicone spatula as they cook, until they're crispy and browned on both sides, about 2 minutes per side. Transfer the browned noodle cakes to the lined plate and sprinkle each one with a pinch of salt. Repeat the process with the remaining noodles, adding more clarified butter to the pan as necessary, so you have 8 crispy cakes.

In another large heavy skillet set over medium-high heat, warm up the pork belly slices (rashers), until they're slightly crispy on the outside but still soft within, about 1 minute on each side.

Evenly divide the noodle cakes, crisp pork belly slices, eggs, and radish salad among 4 plates. We like to do this "diner style" so each component is separate and guests can combine everything however they like. Serve immediately with *sambal oelek* on the side.

Twice-Cooked Pork and Wood Ear Mushroom Omelet

SERVES 4

FOR THE GREEN MANGO SALAD:

1 teaspoon canola (rapeseed)
  or vegetable oil

¼ teaspoon sugar

1½ teaspoons unseasoned rice vinegar

1½ teaspoons fish sauce

1 (12 oz/340 g) green mango, peeled,
  pitted, and cut into thin matchsticks

½ large English cucumber, seeded and
  cut into thin matchsticks

1 large handful Thai basil leaves, torn

Kosher (coarse) salt

FOR THE FILLING:

⅓ oz (20 g) dried wood ear mushrooms

½ lb (230 g) boneless pork shoulder
  (ask your butcher for a single thinly
  sliced piece)

1 teaspoon sugar

1 teaspoon kosher (coarse) salt

2 tablespoons fish sauce, divided

2 tablespoons canola (rapeseed)
  or vegetable oil

½ large white onion, julienned

1 tablespoon sriracha

2 scallions (spring onions), ends trimmed,
  thinly sliced

FOR THE OMELETS:

8 eggs

1 teaspoon kosher (coarse) salt

½ teaspoon black pepper

1 small handful finely chopped herbs
  (cilantro [coriander], Thai basil, parsley,
  tarragon, chives, or a mix)

About 3 tablespoons (45 g) Clarified Butter
  (page 212)

TO SERVE:

2 radishes, thinly sliced

3 tablespoons store-bought crispy fried
  shallots

Fleur de sel

There is something so French about a skillfully prepared omelet. Proper egg cookery is the key—the omelet must be perfectly rolled and evenly cooked without any browning. We fill our omelet with rich, spicy pork, and meaty wood ear mushrooms. The pork—like many types of meat in Vietnamese cooking—benefits from being cooked twice, which adds depth of flavor and can be prepared ahead of time and finished "à la minute". The mango salad lightens up the omelet and makes for a great side dish.

MAKE THE GREEN MANGO SALAD:

In a large bowl, whisk together the oil, sugar, vinegar, and fish sauce until the sugar dissolves. Add the mango, cucumber, and basil and stir gently to combine. Season to taste with salt and set aside.

MAKE THE FILLING:

In a large bowl cover the mushrooms with hot tap water. Place a plate on top to keep the mushrooms submerged, until softened, about 20 minutes.

Meanwhile, place the pork between 2 large pieces of plastic wrap (clingfilm) and, using a mallet, gently pound the pork to tenderize and flatten to about ¼ inch (6 mm) thick. Sprinkle the pork on both sides with the sugar and salt and rub into the meat.

Heat a grill or a grill (griddle) pan set over medium heat. Grill the pork, brushing it while it cooks with 1 tablespoon of the fish sauce, until charred on both sides and firm to the touch, 2 to 3 minutes per side. Transfer the pork to a cutting (chopping) board and let rest while you prepare the mushrooms.

Drain the mushrooms (discard the soaking liquid), then thinly slice and reserve.

Thinly slice the rested pork, discarding any large pieces of fat or sinew.

In a large skillet set over high heat, heat the oil until piping hot, add the sliced pork, and cook, stirring, until the pork is crispy on the edges, about 3 minutes. Add the onion and cook, stirring, until the onion begins to soften and just barely picks up some color, about 5 minutes. Stir in the reserved mushrooms and cook for 1 minute. Add the remaining 1 tablespoon fish sauce and the sriracha and cook just until the liquid evaporates, about 1 minute. Turn off the heat and stir in the scallions. Set aside while you prepare the eggs.

MAKE THE OMELETS:

In a large bowl, whisk together the eggs with the salt and pepper until thoroughly mixed. Stir in the herbs.

Place a small nonstick skillet over medium-high heat and add just enough clarified butter to lightly coat the surface. Add a quarter of the egg mixture and cook, stirring non-stop with a silicone spatula and shaking the pan, until small curds form, 1 to 2 minutes. Stop stirring the omelet for just a few seconds, 10 tops, so the underside sets itself and forms almost a thin skin. Place a quarter of the warm pork filling over half the omelet. Fold the other half of the omelet over, then carefully invert the omelet onto a plate. Cover it to keep warm while you prepare the remaining omelets. Repeat the process 3 more times, adding more butter to the skillet and adjusting the heat as necessary.

TO SERVE:

Shingle the sliced radishes on top of each omelet and sprinkle a pinch of fleur de sel on top of the radishes. Place a quarter of the green mango salad alongside each omelet and sprinkle the crispy fried shallots over each salad. Serve immediately.

Fried Egg, Pork Belly, and Avocado Bánh Mì

MAKES 4 SANDWICHES

½ cup (120 ml) Mayonnaise (page 211) or high-quality store-bought

1 tablespoon *sambal oelek* chile paste

4 (6-inch/15 cm) Bánh Mì Rolls (page 166), high-quality store-bought Vietnamese sandwich rolls, or Mexican *bolillos*

Canola (rapeseed) or vegetable oil, as needed

½ recipe Red Roasted Pork Belly (page 218), sliced thick, or unsmoked slab bacon (streaky), cut into ¼ × 2-inch (5 mm × 5 cm) pieces

1 jalapeño, stemmed and thinly sliced

8 eggs

Kosher (coarse) salt and black pepper

1 ripe Hass avocado, halved, pitted, peeled, and sliced

1 handful of each: cilantro (coriander) and mint leaves

We don't claim to have invented the breakfast *bánh mì*, but we can safely say we had never eaten one before we started making them. This one includes everything great about breakfast: pork, eggs, and avocado. As with all the *bánh mì* we serve, the most important thing is the bread. Unlike a French baguette, which has a hard crust and a dense crumb, a *bánh mì* roll needs a lot of give, should be easy to bite into, and shouldn't compete with the rich fillings. You can make your own Bánh Mì Rolls (page 166), or if you're just looking to make a sandwich, seek out Vietnamese sandwich rolls or Mexican *bolillo* rolls, which have soft interiors and thin, crisp crusts. For a vegetarian version, leave out the pork.

Preheat the oven to 400°F (200°C/Gas Mark 6) or heat the broiler on high.

In a small bowl, whisk together the mayonnaise and *sambal oelek* and reserve the mixture.

Warm the rolls in the oven or under the broiler until the crusts are crisp and the insides are soft and warmed through, a couple of minutes. Cut the rolls almost, but not quite, all the way through and place them, cut side up, on a large work surface. Evenly spread the *sambal oelek* mayonnaise on the cut sides of the rolls.

Warm a slick of oil in a grill (griddle) pan or nonstick pan, add the pork, and cook over medium heat until browned and crispy on each side, about 2 minutes per side. Evenly distribute the pork among the bottom sides of the rolls. Top with the sliced jalapeño.

Add more oil to the pan, if necessary, and, working in batches, crack the eggs into the pan. Season the eggs with salt and pepper and cook until as runny or as well done as you'd like. Transfer the cooked eggs to the sandwiches, using 2 eggs per sandwich. Fan the avocado slices over the eggs and season with salt and pepper. Top each sandwich generously with cilantro and mint. Close the sandwiches, cut each across in half, if you'd like, and serve immediately.

Scrambled Egg, Cilantro, and Jalapeño Bánh Mì

MAKES 4 SANDWICHES

½ cup (120 ml) Mayonnaise (page 211) or high-quality store-bought

1 tablespoon *sambal oelek* chile paste, plus extra for serving

4 (6-inch/15 cm) Bánh Mì Rolls (page 166), high-quality store-bought Vietnamese sandwich rolls, or Mexican *bolillos*

8 eggs

1 teaspoon kosher (coarse) salt

½ teaspoon black pepper

2 tablespoons Clarified Butter (page 212)

2 jalapeños, thinly sliced

2 large handfuls cilantro (coriander) leaves

Sriracha, for serving

Our menu shifts and evolves all the time, but we can't mess with our breakfast *bánh mì* lineup. Our customers are so attached to them that the sandwiches have never changed. This one is the simplest—just eggs, cilantro (coriander), and jalapeño—but it relies on each component holding its own. The eggs must be softly scrambled over not-too-high heat so they don't take on additional color and they have to be cooked in golden clarified butter, which gives them a round, rich flavor. Most important, don't be shy with the jalapeño. This is really a jalapeño and egg sandwich, not the other way around. If jalapeños are too spicy for you, remove the seeds and let the slices soak for a few minutes in ice water to tame the heat. We often add two pork sausage patties from our Sticky Rice with Ginger Sausage, Herb Salad, and Poached Eggs (page 22) to this *bánh mì*, which gives the sandwich a wonderful Jimmy Dean quality. We left them off the recipe for the sake of simplicity and to not overload the breakfast chapter with pork.

Preheat the oven to 400°F (200°C/Gas Mark 6) or heat the broiler on high.

In a small bowl, whisk together the mayonnaise and the *sambal oelek* and reserve the mixture.

Warm the rolls in the oven or under the broiler until the crusts are crisp and the insides are soft and warmed through, a couple of minutes. Cut the rolls almost, but not quite, all the way through and place them, cut side up, on a large work surface. Evenly spread the *sambal oelek* mayonnaise on the cut sides of the rolls.

Meanwhile, place the eggs in a large bowl with the salt and pepper and use a fork to beat the eggs until thoroughly mixed. Place a large nonstick skillet over medium heat and add enough clarified butter to lightly coat the surface. Add the eggs and cook, stirring gently with a silicone spatula, until the eggs are just set but are still creamy, about 3 minutes.

Evenly distribute the eggs among the bottom sides of the rolls. Top with the sliced jalapeños and cilantro. Close the sandwiches, cut each in half across, if you'd like, and serve immediately with extra *sambal oelek* and sriracha on the side.

Egg White, Mushroom, and Fresno Chile Bánh Mì

MAKES 4 SANDWICHES

½ cup (120 ml) Mayonnaise (page 211) or high-quality store-bought

1 tablespoon *sambal oelek* chile paste, plus extra for serving

3 tablespoons canola (rapeseed) or vegetable oil

1 small bunch fresh oyster mushrooms (1½ oz/43 g), tough stems discarded, roughly chopped

6 fresh shiitake mushrooms (3 oz/85 g), stems discarded, roughly chopped

10 fresh white (button) mushrooms (5 oz/140 g), stems discarded, thinly sliced

Kosher (coarse) salt and black pepper

6 scallions (spring onions), ends trimmed, thinly sliced, divided

4 (6-inch/15 cm) Bánh Mì Rolls (page 166), high-quality store-bought Vietnamese sandwich rolls, or Mexican *bolillos*

12 egg whites (reserve the yolks for another use, such as making ice cream or Crispy Vermicelli Cakes with the Works on page 24)

2 tablespoons Clarified Butter (page 212)

1 large handful cilantro (coriander) leaves

1 Fresno or other fresh red chile, stemmed and thinly sliced

This is the lightest of our breakfast *bánh mì* options and the one we eat the most often. With a satisfying combination of sautéed mushrooms and protein-rich egg whites, this sandwich is brightened with fresh cilantro (coriander) and hot chiles. A breakfast sandwich that doesn't put you to sleep is a keeper.

Preheat the oven to 400°F (200°C/Gas Mark 6).

In a small bowl, whisk together the mayonnaise and the *sambal oelek* and reserve the mixture.

Heat the oil in a large nonstick skillet and, when piping hot, add all the mushrooms and cook over high heat, stirring now and then, until browned and softened, about 7 minutes. Season the mushrooms to taste with salt and pepper. Stir in two-thirds of the scallions and use a slotted spoon to transfer the mixture to a plate or bowl and reserve. Wipe out the skillet with a paper towel and set aside.

Warm the rolls in the oven or under the broiler until the crusts are crisp and the insides are soft and warmed through, a couple of minutes. Cut the rolls almost, but not quite, all the way through and place them, cut side up, on a large work surface. Evenly spread the *sambal oelek* mayonnaise on the cut sides of the rolls.

In a large bowl, whisk together the egg whites, 1 teaspoon salt, and ½ teaspoon pepper until thoroughly mixed and slightly frothy. Return the skillet to the stove over medium heat and add the clarified butter. Add the egg whites and cook, stirring gently with a silicone spatula, until the egg whites are just set, about 3 minutes. Stir in the remaining scallions.

Evenly distribute the egg whites among the bottom sides of the rolls and top each sandwich with a quarter of the reserved mushrooms, the cilantro, and the sliced chile. Close the sandwiches, cut each in half across, if you'd like, and serve immediately with extra *sambal oelek* on the side.

Spicy Breakfast Fried Rice and Fried Eggs

SERVES 4

2 tablespoons sriracha

2 tablespoons unseasoned rice vinegar

2 tablespoons fish sauce

¼ cup (60 ml) plus 2 tablespoons canola (rapeseed) or vegetable oil, plus extra as needed

1 yellow onion, finely diced

1 jalapeño, stemmed and minced

1 Fresno or other fresh red chile, stemmed and minced

Kosher (coarse) salt and black pepper

1 small bunch fresh oyster mushrooms (1½ oz/43 g), tough stems discarded, roughly chopped

10 white (button) mushrooms (5 oz/140 g), stems discarded, thinly sliced

4 cups (600 g) cold cooked long-grain white rice (leftover take-out [take-away] rice is perfect for this)

1 cup (100 g) fresh mung bean sprouts

1 large handful cilantro (coriander) leaves, roughly chopped with a handful set aside for garnish

2 scallions (spring onions), ends trimmed, thinly sliced

3 oz (90 g) shishito peppers (about 20 peppers)

4 eggs

While this fried rice isn't on our printed menu, we often prepare variations of it for a special of the day. It's also great with cooked quinoa or any other grain you might have kicking around. The combination of mushrooms and eggs make this a filling vegetarian option, but it would also be delicious with small crispy cubes or slices (rashers) of crisp Red Roasted Pork Belly (page 218). The most important thing here is the slurry of sriracha, rice vinegar, and fish sauce stirred in at the end. The sugar and garlic from sriracha, the acid from vinegar, and the umami from fish sauce all come together to create a sum greater than each individual part.

In a small bowl, whisk together the sriracha, vinegar, and fish sauce. Reserve the mixture.

Heat ¼ cup (60 ml) oil in a large nonstick skillet and, when piping hot, add the onion, jalapeño, Fresno chile, a big pinch of salt, and a few grinds of black pepper and cook over high heat, stirring now and then, until the vegetables begin to soften and just barely begin to brown, about 5 minutes. Add all the mushrooms and season the mixture once again with salt and pepper. Cook, stirring now and then, until the mushrooms are softened and browned in spots, about 5 minutes. Use your hands to crumble in the rice; if it seems dry, add up to 2 tablespoons more oil. Heat the rice, stirring to break up any clumps, until the rice is heated through, about 5 minutes. Stir in the reserved sriracha mixture, the bean sprouts, chopped cilantro, and scallions. Season the rice to taste with salt and keep it warm over very low heat.

Meanwhile, place a large nonstick skillet over high heat and add enough oil to lightly coat the surface. When the oil is piping hot, add the shishito peppers and cook, stirring now and then, until the peppers are softened and charred in spots, about 3 minutes. Season the peppers generously with salt and transfer them to a plate. Wipe out the skillet with a paper towel and then add enough fresh oil to lightly coat the surface. Crack the eggs into the pan and sprinkle each one with a pinch of salt. Cook until the whites are just set and the yolks are still runny, about 3 minutes. To help cook the whites on top, tilt the skillet toward you and use a spoon to collect the hot oil and baste it over the eggs while they set.

Evenly divide the rice among 4 plates or shallow bowls and top each portion with an egg. Divide the shishito peppers among the plates, garnish with cilantro, and serve.

Chicken and Rice Breakfast Soup

SERVES 6

2½ cups (550 g) Thai sticky rice (or any sweet, glutinous rice), rinsed well

12 cups (3 liters) Vietnamese Meat Stock (page 216), made with chicken bones

4 bone-in, skinless chicken thighs

Kosher (coarse) salt

2 scallions (spring onions), ends trimmed, thinly sliced

1 jalapeño, stemmed and thinly sliced, or more to taste

½ large white onion, julienned

1 small handful cilantro (coriander) leaves

Sambal oelek chile paste, for serving (optional)

This cozy chicken soup for the Vietnamese soul is the most comforting way to start the day and one of the best-ever uses of leftover cooked rice. Inspired by congee, the slow-cooked Chinese rice porridge, our version is infused with Vietnamese aromatics. The longer the rice sits in the hot soup, the more liquid it absorbs to become a soupy rice rather than a soup with rice. If you have any soup left over, you might need little additional stock (broth) to stretch the soup out.

Place the rice in a large bowl and cover with cool water. Soak the rice for 15 minutes, stirring now and then, then drain, rinse with fresh water, and reserve.

In a large pot, bring the stock (broth) to a boil. Reduce the heat and simmer, then add the chicken thighs. Cover and cook until the thighs are completely cooked through, 25 minutes. Transfer the thighs to a bowl and let them cool. Season the stock to taste with salt. Add the reserved rice to the stock and simmer until the rice is cooked through, about 15 minutes.

Meanwhile, discard the bones from the chicken and shred the meat. Add the shredded meat to the stock and simmer until the chicken is warmed through, about 2 minutes. Taste the soup for seasoning and divide it among 4 large soup bowls. Garnish each bowl with a quarter of the scallions, jalapeño, onion, and cilantro. Add a little *sambal oelek*, if using. Serve piping hot.

NOTE: If you don't have Vietnamese Meat Stock (page 216), use high-quality store-bought chicken stock and, along with the chicken thighs, add 2 whole cloves, 1 (2-inch/5 cm) cinnamon stick, 1 star anise, 1 (4-inch/10 cm) piece crushed fresh ginger, and 1 (8 × 8-inch/20 × 20 cm) piece dried kombu. Simmer the stock while the chicken cooks, about 25 minutes, then strain through a fine-mesh sieve. Reserve the chicken and discard the remaining solids. Finish with ¼ cup (60 ml) fish sauce and 2 teaspoons palm or granulated sugar when you add the rice.

Bún Bo Hue

SERVES 4

17 cups (4 liters) Vietnamese Meat Stock
   (page 216)

½ lb (230 g) beef brisket, trimmed of
   excess fat

6 oz (170 g) raw beef tendon (about 1 whole
   tendon)

Kosher (coarse) salt

¼ cup (60 ml) canola (rapeseed) or
   vegetable oil

1 white onion, julienned, divided

2 garlic cloves, thinly sliced

1 cup (240 g) tomato paste (purée)

1 cup (240 g) *sambal oelek* chile paste

1 stalk fresh lemongrass (white part only),
   outer layers peeled off, bruised with the
   back of your knife or a mallet

1 large bunch cilantro (coriander)

8 oz (230 g) thick rice noodles (*bún bo
   hue tuoi* noodles)

½ lb (230 g) Red Roasted Pork Belly
   (page 216)

8 spicy pork meatballs (see page 76)

2 tablespoons white shoyu or 1 tablespoon
   soy sauce

6 scallions (spring onions), ends trimmed,
   thinly sliced

Bean sprouts, Thai basil leaves, cilantro
   (coriander) leaves, lime wedges, sliced
   radishes, fish sauce, and ESC Fragrant
   Chile Oil (page 206) or high-quality
   store-bought, for serving

Bún bo hue, a spicy and fortifying soup, makes a memorable and nourishing start to the day. While the tomato paste (purée) isn't a traditionally Vietnamese ingredient, it gives the soup its distinctive brick-red color and a nice depth of flavor. It's vital to get the right type of noodles for this soup: seek out rice noodles marked specifically for *bún bo hue*.

In a large pot, bring the stock (broth) to a boil. Reduce the heat to low and simmer, then add the brisket and tendon. Skim the stock, discarding whatever fat and solids float to the top. Cover the pot, and cook until the brisket is tender, the tendon is gelatinous to the touch, and the stock is fragrant, about 3 hours. Transfer the brisket and tendon to a plate and reserve. Season the stock to taste with salt and turn off the heat.

Meanwhile, heat the oil in a large heavy-bottomed pot, add three-quarters of the onion and all the garlic, and cook over high heat, stirring, until they just begin to soften, about 5 minutes. Reduce the heat to low, add the tomato paste (purée) and *sambal oelek*, and cook, stirring, until the pastes are fragrant and just beginning to brown but not burn, about 6 minutes. Slowly whisk in the reserved stock and add the lemongrass. Tie half of the cilantro together with kitchen twine and add it to the soup. Bring the soup to a boil, then reduce the heat to low while you prepare the noodles.

In a large bowl of cold water, soak the noodles until pliable, about 25 minutes. Meanwhile, bring a pot of lightly salted water to a boil. Drain the noodles in a colander and transfer them to the boiling water. Cook until soft, according to package instructions, on average about 5 minutes. Drain the noodles again, rinse with cold water, and reserve.

Using tongs, discard lemongrass and cilantro from the soup. Slice the reserved brisket and beef tendon, and the pork belly into pieces ¼ inch (.5 cm) thick (trim off and discard any gray or dark spots of beef tendon). Add the sliced meats and tendon to the soup along with the meatballs and cook until warmed through, about 5 minutes. Roughly chop the remaining cilantro and stir it into the soup along with the white shoyu. Taste and adjust seasoning and, if needed, add a bit of warm water if the soup has reduced too much and tastes too concentrated.

Put the reserved noodles into a fine-mesh sieve and dunk them into the soup to warm them. Divide the warm noodles among 4 large soup bowls and ladle the soup over the noodles, evenly distributing the meat. Garnish each bowl with the remaining white onion and the scallions.

Serve immediately with a platter full of bean sprouts, Thai basil leaves, cilantro leaves, lime wedges, sliced radishes, fish sauce, and chile oil.

NOTE: If you don't have Vietnamese Meat Stock (page 216), use high-quality store-bought beef stock and, along with the meats, add 2 whole cloves, 1 (2-inch/5 cm) cinnamon stick, 1 star anise, 1 (4-inch/10 cm) piece crushed fresh ginger, and 1 (8 × 8-inch/20 × 20 cm) piece dried kombu. Simmer the stock while the meat cooks, about 3 hours, then strain the stock through a fine-mesh sieve. Reserve the meat and discard the remaining solids. Season to taste with salt before proceeding with the rest of the recipe.

Breakfast Pho with Poached Eggs

SERVES 4

½ lb (230 g) boneless beef short rib
(preferably in 1 piece)

½ lb (230 g) beef brisket, trimmed
of excess fat

½ lb (230 g) flank steak

Kosher (coarse) salt and black pepper

Canola (rapeseed) or vegetable oil,
as needed

17 cups (4 liters) Vietnamese Meat Stock
(page 216)

14 oz (400 g) fresh *pho* noodles or 8 oz
(230 g) dry

1 tablespoon white or unseasoned
rice vinegar

4 eggs

1 small white onion, julienned

6 scallions (spring onions), ends trimmed,
thinly sliced

Bean sprouts, Thai basil leaves, cilantro
(coriander) leaves, sliced jalapeños,
sliced radishes, lime wedges, fish sauce,
and *sambal oelek* chile paste, for serving

Pho is probably the most well-known Vietnamese dish, and traditionally it is served for breakfast. We like to add a poached egg to our version. When you break open the yolk, it enriches the broth, making it almost like egg-drop soup. After polishing off a bowl of this, you're ready for whatever the day might have in store.

Generously season the short rib, brisket, and flank steak on both sides with salt and pepper. Place a large heavy skillet over high heat and add enough oil to lightly coat the surface. Once the oil is piping hot, place the meats in the skillet and cook, turning each piece of meat once, until deeply browned on both sides but still rare inside, about 2 minutes per side. Work in batches if necessary. Transfer the meats to a plate and reserve.

In a large pot set, bring the stock (broth) to a boil, then reduce the heat and simmer. Pat dry the seared short rib and brisket with a paper towel and transfer them to the pot. Once the flank steak cools, wrap it in plastic wrap and reserve in the refrigerator. Skim the stock, discarding whatever fat and solids float to the top. Cook the stock, covered and over very low heat, until the short rib and brisket are tender and the stock is fragrant, about 2½ hours. Transfer the short rib and brisket to the plate with the flank steak and let the meat cool to room temperature. Strain the stock through a cheesecloth-lined fine-mesh sieve into a clean pot (this will ensure a clear, clean broth). Season the broth to taste with salt and keep it warm over low heat.

Once cool enough to handle, slice the short rib and brisket ¼ inch (.5 cm) thick and add them to the soup to warm through (if you make the meats ahead of time and chill them completely in the refrigerator, they will be even easier to slice thinly). Unwrap the steak, slice it ¼ inch (.5 cm) thick, but do not add to the soup.

Meanwhile, bring 2 separate large pots of lightly salted water to boil. Cook the noodles in one pot until they are al dente (either about 30 seconds for fresh or about 5 minutes for dried, but check the package for precise timing as brands differ). Drain the noodles in a colander. Warm 4 large soup bowls in a 300°F (150°C/Gas Mark 2) oven for 1 minute or in the microwave for 30 seconds. Evenly divide the noodles among the bowls.

Add the vinegar to the other pot and reduce the heat to low. Crack the eggs one at a time into a small bowl. Stir the water gently to create a whirlpool and, while gently stirring, carefully slip the egg into the simmering water. Repeat the process as quickly as possible with the remaining eggs, working in batches as necessary as determined by the size of your pan so that the eggs stay separate. Poach the eggs until they're barely firm to the touch, about 3 minutes. Remove the eggs with a slotted spoon and blot dry on paper towels. Put a poached egg into each of the bowls and distribute the sliced flank steak among the bowls. Ladle the hot soup over the noodles, evenly distributing the meat among the bowls. Garnish each bowl with onion and scallion.

Serve immediately with a platter full of bean sprouts, Thai basil, cilantro, sliced jalapeños, sliced radishes, and lime wedges to add to your *pho* as you like. Make sure there's a bottle of fish sauce and some *sambal oelek* for stirring into your soup, too.

NOTE: If you don't have Vietnamese Meat Stock (page 216) on hand, see *Bún Bo Hue* (page 38) for a shortcut.

Homemade Granola with Yogurt, Ginger, and Palm Sugar Syrup

MAKES 2 CUPS (425 G)

1¼ cups (230 g) steel-cut oats

½ cup (60 g) whole raw macadamia nuts

1 tablespoon roughly chopped crystallized ginger

¼ cup (20 g) unsweetened shredded coconut

4 tablespoons (60 g) butter, melted

2 tablespoons honey

2 tablespoons packed dark brown sugar

½ teaspoon kosher (coarse) salt

2 oz (60 g) palm sugar

1 (2-inch/5 cm) piece fresh ginger, thinly sliced

2 cups (260 g) mixed berries (we use blackberries, raspberries, and blueberries; if you use strawberries, trim and slice them)

2 tablespoons fresh lime juice

1 small handful fresh mint leaves, thinly sliced

2 cups (475 ml) full-fat Greek yogurt or Lebanese labneh

Alex Manley, our original head baker, came up with this crunchy granola full of Southeast Asian flavor from the coconut and ginger. There's an extra hit of ginger in the palm sugar syrup, which is also great when added to lemonade and cocktails. The granola is a versatile snack: you can give it to your kid to take to school, eat it any time of day (including dinner), and it's a great accompaniment to a hike.

Preheat the oven to 350°F (175°C/Gas Mark 4).

Line a sheet pan with a silicone baking mat or parchment paper. Place the oats on the lined sheet pan and bake, stirring now and then, until they are golden and smell nutty and fragrant, about 15 minutes. Transfer the oats to a large bowl and set aside the sheet pan. Turn down the oven to 300°F (150°C/Gas Mark 2).

Meanwhile, place the macadamia nuts and crystallized ginger in a food processor and pulse until finely chopped. Add the nut mixture and coconut to the oats and stir to combine. In a small bowl, whisk together the butter, honey, brown sugar, and salt. Use a silicone spatula to scrape all the butter mixture over the oat mixture and stir to combine. Transfer the mixture to the reserved sheet pan and spread it out so it forms an even layer. Bake the granola, stirring every 10 minutes, until dark brown and crisp, about 35 minutes. Let the granola cool completely (it will continue to crisp as it cools).

Meanwhile, place the palm sugar, ginger, and ½ cup (120 ml) water in a small saucepan set over high heat. Bring the mixture to a boil, then reduce the heat and simmer, stirring to break up and dissolve the palm sugar, until the syrup is quite thick and turns the color of an Irish setter, and the ginger is fragrant, about 10 minutes. Let the syrup cool completely, strain it through a fine-mesh sieve into a small pitcher (jug), and reserve it. Discard the ginger (or reserve for another use or snack on it).

Place the berries, lime juice, and mint in a large bowl and stir to combine. Divide the yogurt among 4 serving bowls and top each bowl with a quarter of the berry mixture. Drizzle each portion of berries with a quarter of the reserved syrup. Place a small handful of granola in each bowl and serve immediately. Store the granola in an airtight container at room temperature for up to 1 week.

Nutella and Banana Crêpes with Candied Hazelnuts

SERVES 4

FOR THE CANDIED HAZELNUTS:

1 cup (200 g) granulated sugar

1 tablespoon light corn syrup

½ cup (80 g) blanched hazelnuts

Canola (rapeseed) or vegetable oil,
   for frying

FOR THE CRÊPES:

2 eggs

¾ cup (180 ml) milk

1 cup (120 g) all-purpose (plain) flour

3 tablespoons (45 g) butter, melted,
   plus extra for cooking

½ teaspoon vanilla extract

¼ teaspoon ground cinnamon

1½ teaspoons granulated sugar

Pinch of kosher (coarse) salt

½ cup (150 g) hazelnut-chocolate spread,
   such as Nutella

2 bananas, peeled and thinly sliced on
   the bias

½ cup (115 g) crème fraîche

Powdered (icing) sugar, for dusting

For our savory Vietnamese crêpe on our lunch menu, we have a bunch of French blue steel crêpe pans. When we saw that the pans weren't getting much use during the morning service, we added an old-school sweet French crêpe to the breakfast menu. If you want to speed up the recipe, the candied hazelnuts can be swapped for roughly chopped toasted hazelnuts.

MAKE THE CANDIED HAZELNUTS:

Place the granulated sugar, corn syrup, and 1 cup (240 ml) water in a small heavy-bottomed pot set over high heat. Bring the mixture to a boil, then reduce the heat to a simmer, and add the hazelnuts. Cook the hazelnuts, stirring, for 30 minutes. Drain the hazelnuts (save the syrup for sweetening your coffee or cocktails) and dry them on paper towels.

Heat 1 inch (2.5 cm) oil in a small heavy-bottomed pot and, once the oil reaches 350°F (175°C) (or a hazelnut sizzles upon contact with the oil), add the hazelnuts and cook over high heat, stirring, until deep golden brown, about 2 minutes. Use a slotted spoon to transfer the nuts to a piece of parchment paper or a wire rack to cool down completely (don't use paper towels because the nuts will stick to it and you will end up eating paper).

MAKE THE CRÊPES:

Place the eggs in a large bowl and whisk until thoroughly combined. Whisk in the milk and ½ cup (120 ml) water and then stir in the flour. Next, stir in the butter, vanilla, cinnamon, granulated sugar, and salt. Let the batter rest for 20 minutes (alternatively, you can refrigerate the batter in an airtight container for up to 2 days and bring it back to room temperature before proceeding).

Place a 12-inch (30 cm) nonstick skillet over medium-high heat and add enough butter to lightly coat the surface. Pour in about a quarter of the batter (about ½ cup/ 120 ml) and swirl the skillet so the batter forms an even layer. Cook, rotating the pan as necessary so the crêpe cooks evenly, until the underside is golden brown, about 2 minutes. Using a large high-heat silicone or wooden spatula and your hands, quickly and confidently flip the crêpe and cook until the second side is golden brown, about 1 more minute. Transfer the crêpe to your work surface and repeat the process 3 more times with the remaining batter, adding more butter to your skillet as needed, so you end up with 4 crêpes.

Spread 2 tablespoons of the hazelnut-chocolate spread over half of each crêpe. Evenly distribute the banana slices among the crêpes, laying them over the center of the spread. Fold each crêpe in half, covering the spread and bananas, to form semicircles. Fold the filled crêpes in half a second time. Transfer the filled crêpes to 4 plates and dollop each with 2 tablespoons of the crème fraîche. Sprinkle a handful of the candied hazelnuts on top of each crêpe, dust with powdered sugar, and serve immediately.

Brioche French Toast with Blueberry Compote and Brown Butter Sauce

SERVES 4

FOR THE BLUEBERRY COMPOTE:

2 cups (260 g) blueberries

¼ cup (50 g) granulated sugar

Pinch of kosher (coarse) salt

10 Thai basil leaves, finely chopped

FOR THE BROWN BUTTER SAUCE:

8 tablespoons (115 g) butter, divided

½ cup (100 g) packed light brown sugar

¼ teaspoon kosher (coarse) salt

¼ cup (60 ml) heavy (whipping) cream

1 tablespoon brandy (optional)

½ teaspoon vanilla extract

FOR THE FRENCH TOAST:

Canola (rapeseed) or vegetable oil,
  for frying

1 small handful Thai basil leaves

1 teaspoon plus 3 tablespoons granulated
  sugar, divided

4 eggs

½ teaspoon ground cinnamon

½ cup (120 ml) milk

¼ cup (60 ml) heavy (whipping) cream

4 (1½-inch/4 cm) thick slices Brioche
  (page 167) or store-bought

2 tablespoons (30 g) butter, plus more
  as needed

4 large scoops Double Vanilla Ice Cream
  (page 144) or store-bought

French toast is one of our most-ordered breakfast dishes. Soaking a large slice of brioche in plenty of custard and finishing it in the oven gives it a puffed texture that has almost a soufflé-like effect. The blueberry compote and brown butter sauce (both of which are great ice cream toppers) are such complementary flavors and form a beautiful marriage. If you don't want to go to the trouble of frying the basil for the garnish, you could add extra chopped basil to the blueberry compote.

MAKE THE BLUEBERRY COMPOTE:

In a small saucepan set over medium-high heat, combine the blueberries, sugar, and salt and bring the mixture to a boil. Reduce the heat and simmer until all the berries have burst and the juice is slightly thickened, about 15 minutes. Turn off the heat and let the compote cool for 10 minutes. Stir in the basil and reserve the compote.

MAKE THE BROWN BUTTER SAUCE:

Place 4 tablespoons (60 g) of the butter in a small saucepan set over high heat. Bring the butter to a boil, swirling (but not stirring) the pan now and then, until the butter turns hazelnut brown, about 4 minutes. Watch closely, as the butter goes from brown to burnt very fast. Immediately add the remaining butter, the brown sugar, salt, heavy cream, brandy (if using), and vanilla. Reduce the heat and simmer the sauce just until the brown sugar is dissolved, about 3 minutes. Keep the sauce warm over low heat.

MAKE THE FRENCH TOAST:

Heat ½ inch (1 cm) of oil in a small saucepan set over medium heat. Make sure the basil leaves are completely dry, then carefully place them in the oil. Stand back as you do this, since herbs are made mostly of water, and the basil will sputter and spit when first placed in the oil. Fry the basil, stirring to separate the leaves, until crisp, about 30 seconds. Use a slotted spoon to transfer the basil to a dry paper towel to drain. Sprinkle the warm, crispy basil with 1 teaspoon of sugar and reserve while you prepare the French toast.

Preheat the oven to 300°F (150°C/Gas Mark 2).

Crack the eggs into a large baking dish (or another wide, rimmed vessel) and whisk until thoroughly combined. Add 2 tablespoons of the remaining sugar and the cinnamon and whisk until completely smooth. Whisk in the milk and cream. Place the brioche into the egg mixture and let the slices sit for a full minute until the undersides are soaked with the mixture. Turn the slices over and let them sit for another minute so the second sides are also thoroughly saturated.

Meanwhile, place a large oven-safe nonstick skillet over medium-high heat and add the butter. Place the brioche slices into the skillet and drizzle whatever egg mixture remains, if any, over the slices. Cook the French toast until the undersides are golden brown, about 3 minutes. Turn the pieces over and then place the whole skillet in the oven until the French toast is browned on the second side, about 10 minutes. (Finishing the French toast in the oven will ensure that all the egg mixture gets cooked through.) If your skillet is not large enough for all 4 pieces, cook the French toast in batches, adding more butter as needed, and finish them on a sheet pan in the oven.

Place the French toast on a serving platter and top each slice with 1 scoop of ice cream. Top with the blueberry compote and brown butter sauce. Garnish with some reserved fried basil and serve immediately.

Croissant Beignets with Raspberry-Lychee Jam

MAKES 60 BEIGNETS
(ABOUT 20 SERVINGS) AND
2 CUPS (475 ML) JAM

FOR THE JAM:

2 (10 oz/284 g) bags frozen raspberries

1 (20 oz/565 g) can lychees, drained and roughly chopped

1½ cups (300 g) granulated sugar

FOR THE BEIGNETS:

1 recipe dough from Classic Croissants (page 170), made up to the point of cutting into triangles and rolled out to ¼ inch (6 mm) thick

Canola (rapeseed) or vegetable oil, for frying

Powdered (icing) sugar, for dusting

We source chicory coffee, one of the most popular types of coffee in Vietnam, for our Vietnamese Iced Coffee (page 186) from the famous Café du Monde in New Orleans, Louisiana. As a nod to Café du Monde, and to celebrate our inspiring trip to New Orleans when we were kicking off Elizabeth Street Café, we serve these beignets made from the croissant dough we always have on hand. Be sure to freeze the beignets before frying them because it helps the delicate layers hold their shape; if the beignets are at room temperature when fried, they pretty much disintegrate. The recipe below makes a generous batch of jam, but it is so delicious and keeps so well that it's worth having extra.

MAKE THE JAM:

In a large pot set over high heat, combine the raspberries, chopped lychees, and sugar and bring the mixture to a boil. Reduce the heat and simmer, stirring now and then, until thick and reduced down to about 2 cups (475 ml), about 1 hour. Transfer the jam to a clean jar and let it cool completely before serving. It will continue to thicken as it cools. Cover and refrigerate any remaining jam for up to 2 weeks.

MAKE THE BEIGNETS:

Line a sheet pan with plastic wrap (clingfilm) or parchment paper. Cut the prepared croissant dough into 2-inch (5 cm) squares, transfer the squares to the lined sheet pan, and drape with a clean kitchen towel. Let the dough rest and rise in a warm spot in your kitchen until just about doubled in size, about 2 hours. The layers should be clearly defined and the dough should be quite pillowy. Transfer the rested squares to the freezer until just solid, about 1 hour (at which point you can transfer them to an airtight bag and freeze for up to 1 month).

Meanwhile, line a plate with paper towels and set aside. Heat 2 inches (5 cm) of oil in a large heavy-bottomed pot set over medium-high heat until it reaches 350°F (175°C), or a tiny piece of dough bubbles vigorously when you place it in the hot oil. Carefully place the beignets, in batches, as determined by the size of your pot so that they are not crowded, into the hot oil. Fry, turning now and then, until golden brown on all sides, about 4 minutes total. Transfer the browned beignets to the lined plate to drain. Dust with plenty of powdered sugar and serve immediately with the reserved jam.

LUNCH

Fresh Crab and Glass Noodle Spring Rolls

MAKES 12 ROLLS

Kosher (coarse) salt

3 oz (85 g) glass noodles

12 rice papers

2 Fresno or other fresh red chiles, stemmed and thinly sliced

1 small handful tarragon leaves

1 small head green leaf lettuce (about 2 large handfuls), thinly sliced

1 cup (110 g) peeled and julienned jicama

1 lb (455 g) high-quality fresh crabmeat, picked over for shells and cartilage

Nuoc Cham (page 208), Sweet Chile Vinegar (page 208), and/or Peanut Sauce (page 206), for serving

Charles Phan, the incredible Vietnamese chef who runs the esteemed Slanted Door restaurant in San Francisco, California, has a recipe that holds a special place in our hearts—glass noodles stir-fried with crab. Former *New York Times* food columnist Mark Bittman made the recipe famous. We reimagined the dish into these refreshing spring rolls that are especially great to eat whenever it's hot out—which, in Austin, is often. Use any type of crab you like as long as it's good and fresh. If you're on the West Coast, sweet Dungeness crab is best, and if you're on the East Coast, blue crab works well. (If you're somewhere in between, use the meat from high-quality frozen king crab claws.)

Bring a large pot of salted water to a boil and cook the glass noodles for 1 minute, stirring gently while they cook to separate them. Drain the noodles in a colander and immediately transfer them to a kitchen towel to dry completely and reach room temperature. Use a pair of scissors to roughly cut the noodles—this will make them easier to divide among the rolls.

Fill a large bowl with room-temperature water and set next to a clean work surface. Working with 1 piece of rice paper at a time, quickly dip the rice paper in the water until it just starts to soften, about 10 seconds. (The rice paper will continue to soften as you make the roll.) Pat the rice paper dry on both sides with a clean cotton dish towel. Put a few slices of Fresno chile and a few leaves of tarragon on the softened rice paper, top with a small handful of the noodles (about ½ oz/15 g), a small pile of lettuce, a bit of the jicama, and a small portion of the crab (about 1¼ oz/35 g). Wrap the spring rolls up tightly, as if it were a small burrito. Repeat the process with the remaining wrappers and fillings. Serve immediately with a bowl of *nuoc cham*, chile vinegar, and/or peanut sauce, for dipping.

Grilled Octopus Salad with Charred Jalapeño and Lemongrass Dressing

SERVES 4

FOR THE OCTOPUS:

1 (2 to 3 lb/1 to 1.3 kg) whole fresh octopus or 2 lb (1 kg) fresh or frozen baby octopus

3 tablespoons canola (rapeseed) or vegetable oil

1 teaspoon dried red chile flakes

½ teaspoon black pepper

2 teaspoons chicken bouillon powder (we prefer the Knorr brand *caldo de pollo*)

1 large shallot or small white onion, quartered

1 large carrot, roughly chopped

1 tablespoon minced fresh ginger

1 garlic clove, minced

FOR THE DRESSING:

1 jalapeño, stemmed

1 stalk fresh lemongrass (white part only), outer layers peeled off, bruised with the back of your knife or a mallet and roughly chopped

3 tablespoons unseasoned rice vinegar

1 small garlic clove, minced

2 teaspoons minced shallot

1 teaspoon fish sauce

1½ tablespoons canola (rapeseed) or vegetable oil

Kosher (coarse) salt

FOR THE SALAD:

3 tablespoons extra-virgin olive oil, divided

Kosher (coarse) salt and black pepper

1 teaspoon fish sauce

2 medium kohlrabi (about ½ lb/230 g), peeled and cut into thin matchsticks

½ large jicama (about ½ lb/230 g), peeled and cut into thin matchsticks

6 large radishes, cut into thin rounds

2 large handfuls mint leaves, torn

3 scallions (spring onions), ends trimmed, thinly sliced

1 small handful cilantro (coriander) leaves, roughly chopped

1 large handful store-bought crispy fried shallots

When we put this salad on the menu, it became so popular that we had to devise a consistent way to cook the octopus perfectly each and every time. We like to blanch our octopus quickly and then park it in the oven with aromatics and our secret ingredient—Mexican *caldo de pollo* (a dried bouillon powder). The blanching helps break down the octopus proteins to make it tender, and the bouillon powder makes it flavorful. You can buy precooked Japanese octopus in the freezer section of Asian grocery stores, if you can't find it fresh.

MAKE THE OCTOPUS:
Preheat the oven to 400°F (200°C/Gas Mark 6).

Fill a pot large enough to accommodate your octopus with water and bring it to a boil. Add the octopus, making sure it's fully submerged, and cook for 1 minute (or 3 minutes if using frozen baby octopus). Transfer the octopus to a cutting (chopping) board and let it rest until cool enough to handle. Once cool, using scissors or a knife, remove the tentacles from the center of the octopus (the head) and place them in a nonreactive baking dish. (If using baby octopus, use scissors to cut off the heads and cut the bodies in half.) Discard the head(s).

Drizzle the oil over the octopus and sprinkle with the chile flakes, pepper, and bouillon powder (or crumble the bouillon cube). Add the shallot, carrot, ginger, and garlic to the baking dish and use your hands to mix the ingredients together.

Cover the baking dish tightly with plastic wrap (clingfilm) and then cover the plastic wrap tightly with aluminum foil. Transfer the octopus to the oven and roast until tender (test with a paring knife), 1 hour for baby octopus or 3 hours for the whole, large tentacles. Transfer the octopus to a cutting board, being careful not to tear the purple outer layer on the tentacles, and cool to room temperature. (Discard the cooking liquid and the aromatics or reserve for a base for a seafood soup or stew). At this point, the octopus can be stored in an airtight container in the refrigerator for up to 3 days.

MAKE THE DRESSING:
If you have a gas stove, char the jalapeño over a high flame, turning it with tongs, until the skin is blackened all over, a few minutes. (Alternatively, broil the pepper, turning it once, until the skin is blackened on both sides, about 15 minutes.) Transfer the pepper to a bowl and cover tightly with plastic wrap until the pepper cools to room temperature.

Meanwhile, place the lemongrass in a small pot with the vinegar. Bring the mixture to a boil, turn off the heat, and let it sit for 20 minutes. Discard the lemongrass and transfer the fragrant vinegar to a small bowl.

Peel and seed the jalapeño under running water. Mince the jalapeño and transfer it to the vinegar along with the garlic, shallot, and fish sauce. Whisk all the ingredients together and, while whisking, slowly drizzle in the oil. Season the dressing to taste with salt and reserve.

MAKE THE SALAD:
Preheat a grill or a grill (griddle) pan over high heat.

Cut the reserved octopus tentacles into 4-inch (10 cm) pieces and cut each piece down the middle (if using baby octopus, leave them as they are). Drizzle the octopus with 2 tablespoons olive oil and season on all sides with salt and pepper. Grill the tentacles just on the white side (the part you exposed when you split the tentacles) until charred and marked, 1 to 2 minutes (if using baby octopus, grill on both sides). Transfer the grilled octopus to a large bowl and drizzle with the remaining olive oil and the fish sauce. Toss to combine and let the octopus rest until barely warm.

Add the kohlrabi, jicama, radishes, mint, scallions, cilantro, and reserved dressing to the octopus and toss gently to combine. Transfer to a serving bowl and sprinkle with the fried shallots. Serve immediately.

Glass Noodle and
Seared Flank Steak Salad

SERVES 4 TO 6

FOR THE DRESSING:

½ cup (120 ml) white shoyu or ¼ cup
   (60 ml) regular soy sauce

¼ cup (60 ml) fish sauce

Finely grated zest of 1 lemon

¼ cup (60 ml) fresh lemon juice

¼ cup (60 ml) unseasoned rice vinegar

1 teaspoon sugar

FOR THE SALAD:

2 tablespoons fish sauce

2 tablespoons sugar

1 lb (455 g) flank steak

8 scallions (spring onions), ends trimmed,
   thinly sliced, divided

Kosher (coarse) salt

10 oz (285 g) glass noodles

2 tablespoons extra-virgin olive oil

Black pepper

4 large handfuls baby spinach

¼ cup (60 ml) canola (rapeseed) or
   vegetable oil

2 jalapeños, stemmed and thinly sliced

2 Fresno or other fresh red chiles, stemmed
   and thinly sliced

3 garlic cloves, thinly sliced

1 large shallot, thinly sliced into rings

2 large handfuls cilantro (coriander) leaves
   and stems, roughly chopped

2 large handfuls Thai basil leaves, roughly
   chopped

Marinated Hon Shimeji Mushrooms
   (page 212) with their liquid

1 large handful dill, roughly chopped

1 large handful store-bought crispy
   fried shallots

This salad is hearty enough to make for a great lunch. Because it holds up well, it's an excellent dish to make ahead. When you cook the flank steak, the more charred on the outside and rare on the inside, the better.

MAKE THE DRESSING:

Place the shoyu, fish sauce, lemon zest and juice, vinegar, and sugar in a small bowl and whisk to combine. Reserve the dressing.

MAKE THE SALAD:

In a medium bowl, whisk together the fish sauce, sugar, and 2 tablespoons water until the sugar is dissolved. Pour the mixture into a large resealable plastic bag and add the steak and one-third of the scallions. Squeeze all the air out of the bag so the marinade completely covers the steak. Place the bag in the refrigerator and let the steak marinate for at least 3 hours and up to overnight.

Bring a large pot of salted water to a boil and cook the glass noodles for 1 minute, stirring gently while they cook to separate them. Drain the noodles and immediately transfer them to a kitchen towel to dry completely and reach room temperature. Use a pair of scissors to roughly cut the noodles into pieces 8 inches (20 cm) long—this will make them easier to handle later.

Heat a grill or grill (griddle) pan over very high heat. Remove the steak from the marinade, brush off the scallions, and pat the steak dry with paper towels. Transfer the steak to a plate (or another clean surface), drizzle both sides with the olive oil, and season both sides with pepper. Grill the steak until nicely charred on both sides but still quite soft to the touch and rare in the middle, 2 to 3 minutes per side. (If you prefer it more well done, cook for a few extra minutes on each side.) Transfer the steak to a plate and let it rest for at least 10 minutes before slicing it against the grain into ¼-inch (6 mm) slices. Reserve the steak.

Place the spinach in a large bowl. Heat the canola oil in a large nonstick skillet, and once piping hot, add the jalapeños, Fresno chiles, garlic, and shallot and cook over medium-high heat, stirring, until softened but not browned, about 2 minutes. Reduce the heat to low and add the noodles (if the pan is too hot, they will stick) along with the reserved dressing, and stir to coat the noodles. Immediately transfer the noodles on top of the spinach in the bowl and give 1 minute for the hot noodles to wilt the spinach. Add the cilantro, basil, mushrooms and their liquid, the reserved sliced flank steak, and the remaining sliced scallions and use to tongs to mix the ingredients together. Transfer the noodles to a serving platter (or to individual shallow bowls) and sprinkle with the dill and crispy shallots. Serve while warm or at room temperature.

Cold Beef Tendon with Fish Sauce-Pickled Peppers

SERVES 4

FOR THE PICKLED PEPPERS:

½ lb (225 g) assorted small chiles, halved lengthwise
1 large garlic clove, thinly sliced
1 small shallot, thinly sliced into rings
5 tablespoons unseasoned rice vinegar
1 tablespoon plus 1 teaspoon fish sauce
¼ teaspoon sugar

FOR THE BEEF TENDON:

4 garlic cloves, crushed
1 white onion, quartered
1 (3-inch/7.5 cm) piece fresh ginger, crushed
1 tablespoon black peppercorns
2 tablespoons kosher (coarse) salt
1 lb (455 g) raw beef tendon (about 2 whole tendons)
¼ cup (60 ml) ESC Fragrant Chile Oil (page 206) or high-quality store-bought
Fleur de sel
2 large handfuls cilantro (coriander) leaves

Beef tendon, while not used frequently enough in Western cooking, is popular in northern Vietnamese and Szechuan cuisine—look for it at your local Asian grocery store or ask your butcher. Beef tendon is pleasantly chewy and its neutral taste makes it perfect to showcase whatever you dress it with. Enter our favorite pickled peppers. We always use a mix of small peppers that we grow in planters behind our restaurant and find it's best to use one part spicy Thai bird chiles mixed with three parts mild shishitos. Extra pickled peppers can go into stir-fries, noodle salads, and sandwiches.

MAKE THE PICKLED PEPPERS:

If the peppers are larger than bite size, roughly chop them. (If you'd like the final product to be not too spicy, discard the seeds.) Put the peppers into a medium non-reactive container with the garlic and shallot.

Place the vinegar, fish sauce, sugar, and ¼ cup (60 ml) water in a small pot and bring to a boil. Stir to dissolve the sugar, then pour the hot liquid over the peppers. Place a small bowl or ramekin on top of the peppers to weigh them down so they're completely submerged. Let the peppers sit and cool to room temperature, about 30 minutes. Remove the bowl, cover the container, and refrigerate the peppers until cold, about 2 hours. The peppers can be made up to 2 weeks in advance.

MAKE THE BEEF TENDON:

Place the garlic, onion, ginger, peppercorns, salt, and 8 cups (2 liters) cold water in a large pot and bring to a boil. Reduce the heat to a simmer, add the beef tendons, and cook, turning the tendons now and then, until they are gnarled-looking and gelatinous to the touch, about 3 hours. Transfer the tendons to a plate and let them cool to room temperature. Discard the cooking liquid or reserve for another use such as adding to soup or stocks. (It's especially good in Bún Bo Hue [page 38], since its high amount of collagen will make the tendons rich; note that the liquid freezes well.) Wrap the cooled tendons tightly in plastic wrap (clingfilm) and transfer them to the refrigerator to thoroughly chill, at least 2 hours and up to 3 days.

Unwrap the tendons and trim off and discard any gray or dark spots. Slice the cleaned tendon as thinly as possible and evenly divide the slices among 4 plates, laying them flat on the plate and slightly overlapping them so they cover the surface of the plate (like carpaccio). Evenly divide the pickled peppers among the plates, scattering them over the surface of the beef tendon. Drizzle each plate with about 1 tablespoon of the pickling liquid and 1 tablespoon of the chile oil. Sprinkle each with a pinch of fleur de sel. Top with the cilantro and serve immediately.

Steamed Buns, Just the Buns

MAKES 8 BUNS

1 tablespoon sugar

1 teaspoon active dry yeast

1¼ cups (150 g) bleached all-purpose (plain) flour, plus extra for dusting

2 teaspoons nonfat milk powder

¼ teaspoon baking powder

¼ teaspoon baking soda (bicarbonate of soda)

2 tablespoons vegetable shortening, plus extra for greasing

1 teaspoon kosher (coarse) salt

2 tablespoons canola (rapeseed) or vegetable oil, for brushing

Distilled water, for steaming (optional)

Thanks to David Chang (the prolific and respected chef behind the Momofuku restaurant group), steamed buns became so popular in contemporary Asian-American restaurants that we couldn't resist adding them to our menu. Now they are probably our bestselling item. Endlessly versatile, these buns are good when filled with anything from traditional pork belly (page 69) to fried chicken infused with Kaffir lime (opposite page) to tofu and avocado (page 66). The buns are easy to make and eclipse anything from a commercial freezer. A couple tips: opt for a stainless-steel rather than a bamboo steamer. This will impart a sandy-blond color to the buns. Also, try to use distilled water in the steamer, as it will keep the buns' appearance as pristine as possible.

Place the sugar, yeast, and ¼ cup plus 1 tablespoon (75 ml) lukewarm water in a large bowl and stir together. Let the mixture sit until the surface is foamy and there are a few bubbles (this means that the yeast is working), about 10 minutes. Add the flour, milk powder, baking powder, baking soda, and shortening and use a spoon to mix until a rough dough forms. Add the salt to the dough and work it in with the spoon or with your hands. If the mixture is too dry for the dough to gather together, add 1 tablespoon of water.

Dust your work surface lightly with flour and transfer the dough to it. Shape the dough into a ball and vigorously knead it (press it with the heel of your hand and push it away from you and then pull the dough back onto itself and repeat this over and over) until it is smooth and elastic, about 5 minutes.

Coat the inside of a bowl with a little shortening and transfer the dough to it. Cover the bowl with a kitchen towel or plastic wrap (clingfilm) and set it aside to let the glutens relax, about 45 minutes. Because this dough is dense, it won't rise much, so don't worry if it doesn't double in size like other yeasted doughs.

Line a sheet pan with parchment paper and set aside.

Transfer the dough to a clean work surface and divide it into 8 equal portions. Roll each portion into a ball and then cover the dough balls with a kitchen towel or plastic wrap and let them rest for 10 minutes to let the glutens relax (this will make them easier to shape). Use a rolling pin to roll each rested ball into a long oval about 4 inches (10 cm) long and brush each dough oval with a little oil and then fold each oval in half crosswise.

Transfer the buns to the lined sheet pan and cover loosely with plastic wrap. Let the dough rest until not quite doubled in size but puffed, about 1 hour.

Set up a conventional stainless-steel steamer with distilled water (if using) or tap water. Bring the water to a boil and line the steamer with parchment paper. Working in batches as necessary, so you don't crowd the steamer, transfer the risen buns to the steamer, cover, and steam the buns until they have a bit of sheen on their surface, are puffed, and firm to the touch, about 9 minutes.

Split the buns (brushing them with oil earlier should make this easy) and fill with whatever fillings you like and serve immediately. (If you have any leftover buns or want to make them ahead, cool them down after steaming and then wrap them in plastic wrap and freeze for up to 1 month. Simply reheat the buns for a few minutes in a steamer until warm.)

Kaffir Lime-Fried Chicken Steamed Buns

MAKES 8 BUNS

FOR THE CHICKEN:

1 cup (240 ml) well-shaken full-fat
    coconut milk

12 fresh Kaffir lime leaves

4 scallions (spring onions), ends trimmed,
    roughly chopped

2 garlic cloves, minced

2 tablespoons fish sauce

Finely grated zest and juice of 1 lime

¾ lb (340 g) boneless, skinless chicken
    thighs, large pieces of fat trimmed,
    cut into 1-inch (2.5 cm) pieces

Canola (rapeseed) or vegetable oil,
    for frying

2 cups (240 g) all-purpose (plain) flour

Kosher (coarse) salt

FOR THE BUNS:

3 tablespoons hoisin sauce

1 tablespoon unseasoned rice vinegar

2 tablespoons sriracha, plus extra
    for serving

8 Steamed Buns, Just the Buns (page 64)

¼ cup (60 ml) Fish Sauce Caramel
    (page 212)

½ English cucumber, seeded and cut into
    thick wedges

1 large handful cilantro (coriander) leaves

1 large handful mint leaves

1 Fresno or other fresh red chile, stemmed
    and thinly sliced

The crispy and juicy pieces of chicken thighs in these addictive steamed buns are really just amazing chicken nuggets. We drizzle the fried chicken with Fish Sauce Caramel (page 212), much like you would drizzle honey on Southern fried chicken. It should come as no surprise that kids love these as much as adults do.

MAKE THE CHICKEN:

Combine the coconut milk, Kaffir lime leaves, scallions, garlic, and fish sauce in a blender and process until the Kaffir lime leaves are almost fully puréed with no large pieces. Add the lime zest and juice and purée to combine. Pour the mixture into a large resealable plastic bag and add the chicken. Squeeze all the air out of the bag so the marinade completely covers the chicken and refrigerate for 24 hours.

Preheat the oven to 275°F (140°C/Gas Mark 1). Place a metal wire rack in a sheet pan and set aside.

Heat 1 inch (2.5 cm) of oil in a large heavy-bottomed pot set over medium-high heat.

Put the flour in a baking dish (or another shallow container), add 2 teaspoons of salt, and whisk together. Take the chicken pieces out of the bag, letting the excess marinade drip back into the bag, and dredge them in the flour mixture. Knock off excess flour and carefully place a piece of chicken in the oil to check the temperature. If the oil bubbles vigorously around the chicken, you're ready to fry; if it doesn't, increase the heat and wait until it does. Once the oil is at the right temperature, place the rest of the chicken pieces in the hot oil, working in batches as necessary to avoid crowding the pot. Discard whatever marinade and flour remain. Fry the chicken, turning each piece once, until deep golden brown on both sides, about 2 minutes per side.

Transfer the chicken to the prepared sheet pan and sprinkle each piece with a small pinch of salt. Keep the chicken pieces warm in the oven while you prepare the buns.

ASSEMBLE THE BUNS:

In a small bowl, whisk together the hoisin, vinegar, and sriracha. Open up each steamed bun and spread the hoisin mixture over the surface of the bottom of each bun. Divide the chicken among the buns (each one should get about 2 pieces). Drizzle the fish sauce caramel evenly over the chicken in each bun, then top each one with a wedge of cucumber, some cilantro, mint, and sliced chile. Close the buns and serve immediately with extra sriracha on the side.

Spicy Tofu and Avocado Steamed Buns

MAKES 8

Our go-to vegetarian filling for steamed buns, this is a satisfying combination of spicy tofu and creamy avocado. The tofu is just as good warm as it is at room temperature, so these are great for lunch boxes.

FOR THE TOFU:

1 tablespoon unseasoned rice vinegar

3 tablespoons canola (rapeseed) or vegetable oil, divided

2 tablespoons *sambal oelek* chile paste

1½ tablespoons minced fresh ginger

½ stalk fresh lemongrass (white part only), outer layers peeled off, finely minced

½ teaspoon kosher (coarse) salt

7 oz (200 g) firm tofu, cut into 8 squares

FOR THE BUNS:

3 tablespoons hoisin sauce

1 tablespoon unseasoned rice vinegar

2 tablespoons sriracha, plus extra for serving

8 Steamed Buns, Just the Buns (page 64)

1 ripe Hass avocado, halved, pitted, peeled, and thinly sliced

Kosher (coarse) salt and black pepper

1 large handful cilantro (coriander) leaves

1 large handful mint leaves

1 Fresno or other fresh red chile, stemmed and thinly sliced

MAKE THE TOFU:

In a large bowl, whisk together the vinegar, 2 tablespoons of the oil, the *sambal oelek*, ginger, lemongrass, and salt. Pour the mixture into a large resealable plastic bag and add the tofu. Squeeze all the air out of the bag so that the marinade is completely covering the tofu pieces. Refrigerate the tofu in the refrigerator and let the tofu marinate for at least 3 hours and up to overnight.

Heat the remaining 1 tablespoon oil in a large nonstick skillet set over medium-high heat. Remove the tofu from its marinade, letting any excess drip back into the bag, and place the tofu in the skillet. Cook until golden brown on each side, about 2 minutes per side. Transfer the tofu to a plate and reserve.

ASSEMBLE THE BUNS:

In a small bowl, whisk together the hoisin, vinegar, and sriracha. Open up each steamed bun and spread the hoisin mixture over the surface of the bottom of each bun. Top with 1 slice of the reserved tofu on each bun and divide the avocado slices among the buns. Season each portion with a pinch of salt and black pepper, and top each with some of the cilantro, mint, and sliced chile. Close the buns and serve immediately with extra sriracha on the side.

Green Mango and Cucumber Salad with Spiced Tiny Shrimp

SERVES 4

2 tablespoons tiny dried shrimp (prawns)

½ cup (120 ml) plus 1 teaspoon canola (rapeseed) or vegetable oil

Kosher (coarse) salt

½ teaspoon *gochugaru* (Korean chile powder) or any kind of fine red chile flakes, divided

½ teaspoon finely grated lime zest, plus extra for serving

¼ teaspoon sugar

1½ teaspoons unseasoned rice vinegar

1½ teaspoons fish sauce

1 medium carrot, cut into thin matchsticks

½ large English cucumber, seeded and cut into thin matchsticks

1 green mango (about ¾ lb/340 g), peeled, pitted, and cut into thin matchsticks

1 large handful Thai basil leaves

1 large handful cilantro (coriander) leaves

1 scallion (spring onion), ends trimmed, cut into matchsticks

Black pepper

Small handful dry unsmoked beef jerky, torn or sliced into small pieces (optional)

This salad is one of the more traditional Southeast Asian offerings on our menu. It can be made with any shredded root, like carrots or kohlrabi if you can't find unripe hard green mangoes. You can serve the salad as a bright, light start to a meal or a side to one of our more substantial items (think of it as Vietnamese coleslaw). The spiced shrimp (prawns), just like fish sauce, are a little strong on their own, but add great flavor and crunch to something else. We threw in house-made beef jerky, because it adds another layer of salty, substantial flavor—you can substitute unsmoked beef jerky (or skip it if you don't eat meat). If you place the shredded scallion (spring onion) in the ice water for five minutes, it will curl and get crispier.

In a small bowl, cover the shrimp with warm water and soak until softened, about 10 minutes. Drain the shrimp and transfer them to a paper towel to dry off.

Meanwhile, line a small bowl with paper towels and set aside. Warm the ½ cup (120 ml) oil in a small pot and, once the oil reaches 325°F (160°C) (or a shrimp sizzles upon contact), fry the shrimp over medium-high heat, stirring, until their color deepens and they're crispy, about 3 minutes. Regulate the heat while frying so the shrimp don't burn. Use a slotted spoon to transfer the shrimp to the lined bowl to drain, then discard the paper towel. While the shrimp are still warm, add a pinch of salt, ¼ teaspoon of the *gochugaru*, and the lime zest to the bowl and stir to combine. Reserve the shrimp while you prepare the rest of the salad. Save the cooking oil for another use or discard.

In a large bowl, combine the remaining 1 teaspoon oil and ¼ teaspoon *gochugaru* with the sugar, vinegar, and fish sauce. Whisk until the sugar dissolves. Add the carrot, cucumber, green mango, Thai basil, cilantro, and scallion and stir gently to combine. Season the vegetables to taste with salt and pepper, and sprinkle with a little extra grated lime zest.

Transfer the salad to a serving bowl or platter and sprinkle with the crispy shrimp and the beef jerky (if using). Serve immediately.

Pork Belly Steamed Buns

MAKES 8 BUNS

½ English cucumber, seeded and cut into thick wedges

½ teaspoon kosher (coarse) salt

½ teaspoon sugar

1 tablespoon distilled white vinegar

4 (½-inch/13 mm) slices (rashers) Red Roasted Pork Belly (page 218), halved

3 tablespoons hoisin sauce

1 tablespoon unseasoned rice vinegar

2 tablespoons sriracha, plus extra for serving

8 Steamed Buns, Just the Buns (page 64)

1 large handful cilantro (coriander) leaves

1 large handful mint leaves

This version of a steamed bun is the most traditional. You can find them all over Taiwan, where steamed buns originated. Our take is a bit less greasy and heavy than typical pork belly steamed buns, and is more representative of the lightness of Vietnamese cooking in general. It is filled with fresh herbs, crisp cucumber, and roasted pork belly.

Place the cucumber wedges in a large bowl and sprinkle with the salt and sugar. Add the distilled vinegar and 1 tablespoon water and mix together. Let the cucumbers marinate while you prepare the buns.

Place a large heavy skillet over medium-high heat and, when hot, place the pork belly slices in the skillet and cook, turning once, just to warm each side but still keep the pork nice and soft, about 30 seconds per side. Turn the heat off while you assemble the buns.

In a small bowl, whisk together the hoisin, vinegar, and sriracha. Open each steamed bun and divide the pork belly slices among them. Drizzle each piece of pork belly with some hoisin mixture, then top each one with a wedge of marinated cucumber, cilantro, and mint. Close the buns and serve immediately with extra sriracha on the side.

Mushroom and Spicy Tofu Bún

SERVES 4

FOR THE TOFU:

2 tablespoons unseasoned rice vinegar

¼ cup (60 ml) canola (rapeseed)
  or vegetable oil

¼ cup (60 ml) *sambal oelek* chile paste

3 tablespoons minced fresh ginger

1 stalk fresh lemongrass (white part only),
  outer layers peeled off, finely minced

1 teaspoon kosher (coarse) salt

14 oz (400 g) firm tofu, cut into 8 squares

FOR THE BÚN:

8 oz (230 g) rice vermicelli

3 tablespoons canola (rapeseed)
  or vegetable oil

1 small bunch fresh oyster mushrooms
  (about 1½ oz/45 g), tough stems
  discarded, roughly chopped

6 fresh shiitake mushrooms, stems
  discarded, roughly chopped

10 fresh white (button) mushrooms, stems
  discarded, thinly sliced

Black pepper

6 scallions (spring onions), ends trimmed,
  thinly sliced

½ large head iceberg lettuce, shredded

1 medium carrot, cut into thin matchsticks

1 English cucumber, peeled and thinly
  sliced

2 jalapeños, stemmed and thinly sliced

4 radishes (preferably breakfast radishes),
  thinly sliced

¼ cup (30 g) dry roasted peanuts, roughly
  chopped (optional)

1 large handful Thai basil leaves

1 large handful cilantro (coriander) leaves

12 mint leaves

2 ripe Hass avocados, halved, pitted,
  peeled, and sliced (optional)

2 tablespoons extra-virgin olive oil

Fleur de sel

1 cup (240 ml) Vegan Nuoc Cham
  (page 208), for serving

Bún, which refers to boiled sticky rice noodles on top of shredded lettuce with a variety of toppings, is the quintessential Vietnamese quick lunch. While *bún* reminds us of summer, it's delicious year-round when you want to eat something light and refreshing but more filling than a green salad. While the toppings vary, lots of fresh vegetables, herbs, and *nuoc cham* sauce are the constants. You can use a zester to partially peel the cucumber (or a peeler to cut stripes on the exterior) to give a striped effect to your cucumber slices.

MARINATE THE TOFU:

In a large bowl, whisk together the vinegar, canola oil, the *sambal oelek*, ginger, lemon-grass, and 1 teaspoon salt. Pour the mixture into a large resealable plastic bag and add the tofu. Squeeze all the air out of the bag so that the marinade is completely covering the tofu pieces. Place the bag in the refrigerator and let the tofu marinate for at least 3 hours and up to overnight.

MAKE THE BÚN:

Bring a medium pot of water to a boil and cook the rice noodles for exactly 4 minutes, stirring gently while they cook to separate them. Drain the noodles in a colander and rinse with cool water to wash off the extra starch. Let the noodles sit for 15 minutes so the excess water drains and the noodles come to room temperature—they should be a little sticky.

Heat the oil in a large nonstick sauté pan set over high heat until smoking. Add all the mushrooms and cook, stirring now and then, until browned and softened, about 7 minutes. Season the mushrooms to taste with salt and pepper. Stir in the scallions and use a slotted spoon to transfer the vegetables to a plate or bowl.

Pour off and discard any excess oil from the pan and return it to the stove over medium heat. Transfer the tofu from its marinade, letting any excess drip back into the bag, to the pan and cook until golden brown on each side, about 1 minute per side, for a total of 6 minutes. Transfer the tofu to a plate and reserve it.

Divide the lettuce among 4 shallow soup or salad bowls and top each one with a quarter of the noodles. Arrange the carrot, cucumber, jalapeños, and radishes around the noodles in little bunches. Sprinkle the peanuts over the noodles, if using, and spoon the reserved mushrooms into 4 small bowls. Place 2 pieces of tofu on each of the 4 small plates. Divide the basil, cilantro, mint, and avocado, if using, among the bowls in neat piles. Drizzle each bowl with a little olive oil and sprinkle each one with a pinch of *fleur de sel.* Divide the *nuoc cham* among 4 small bowls and serve them along with the *bún*, mushrooms, and tofu. As you eat, pour a little *nuoc cham* on your *bún*.

Crispy Pan-Seared Gulf Snapper Bún

SERVES 4

8 oz (230 g) rice vermicelli

4 (6 oz/170 g) fillets gulf snapper or any lean fish with firm, white flesh

Kosher (coarse) salt and black pepper

6 tablespoons extra-virgin olive oil, divided

½ large head iceberg lettuce, shredded

1 medium carrot, cut into thin matchsticks

1 English cucumber, peeled and thinly sliced

2 jalapeños, stemmed and thinly sliced

4 radishes (preferably breakfast radishes), thinly sliced

2 large handfuls soft herb leaves (a mix of Thai basil, cilantro [coriander], and mint is best)

¼ cup (30 g) dry roasted peanuts, roughly chopped (optional)

3 tablespoons fish sauce

Fleur de sel

1 cup (240 ml) Nuoc Cham (page 208), for serving

Many of the recipes for Elizabeth Street Café were developed right after we got Perla's, our seafood-centric restaurant, off the ground. We were obsessed with figuring out the best ways to cook fish and shellfish, especially all the great types that come from the Gulf Coast. Searing the snapper without any hesitation is the key to this recipe. The fish, with fish sauce and olive oil, is the jewel on top of this *bún*. It's especially great for dinner parties because you can set up the bowls and prepare the *nuoc cham* ahead of time, and then cook the fish just before you and your friends sit down to eat.

Bring a medium pot of water to a boil and cook the rice noodles for exactly 4 minutes, stirring gently while they cook to separate them. Drain the noodles in a colander and rinse with cool water to wash off the extra starch. Let them sit for 15 minutes so the excess water drains and the noodles come to room temperature—they should be a little sticky.

Season both sides of each piece of snapper with salt and pepper. Place 2 tablespoons of the oil in a large heavy skillet set over high heat until piping hot. Add the snapper, skin side down, and cook for 1 minute over high heat. Reduce the heat to medium and continue to cook the fish on the skin side until the skin is crispy and the flesh is firm to the touch and completely opaque, about 5 minutes (depending on the thickness of the fish). Turn off the heat and gently turn each piece of fish over to reveal the crispy skin and to just "kiss" the flesh with the residual heat from the pan. Let the fish rest in the pan off the heat while you set up your bowls.

Divide the lettuce among 4 shallow soup or salad bowls and top each one with a quarter of the noodles. Arrange the carrot, cucumber, jalapeños, radishes, and herbs around the noodles in little bunches. Sprinkle the peanuts over the noodles, if using. Place a piece of snapper, crispy skin side up, in each bowl. Drizzle the fish evenly with the remaining 4 tablespoons oil and the fish sauce. Sprinkle each bowl with a pinch of fleur de sel. Divide the *nuoc cham* among 4 small bowls and serve with the *bún*. As you eat, pour a little *nuoc cham* on your *bún*.

Short Rib and Spicy House Kimchee Bánh Mì

MAKES 4 SANDWICHES

4 cups (1 liter) Vietnamese Meat Stock (page 216)

1 to 2 lb (455 g to 1 kg) boneless beef short rib (less if lean, more if fatty, and preferably in 1 piece)

Kosher (coarse) salt and black pepper

Canola (rapeseed) or vegetable oil, as needed

4 (6-inch/15 cm) Bánh Mì Rolls (page 166), or high-quality store-bought Vietnamese sandwich rolls or Mexican *bolillos*

½ cup (120 ml) Mayonnaise (page 211) or high-quality store-bought

1 tablespoon *sambal oelek* chile paste

2 cups (370 g) drained Spicy House Kimchee (page 215) or high-quality store-bought

2 large handfuls cilantro (coriander) leaves

Will, our general manager at ESC, is Korean, and we're always comparing notes about the Korean cooking he grew up with and all the Vietnamese flavors and techniques that we love. One day we were talking about *galbi*, the delicious short ribs that are so popular in Korean kitchens, and about how many short ribs we use to prepare *pho*. This short rib connection led to a conversation about how great kimchee would be on a *bánh mì* in place of the expected pickled daikon and carrots.

In a large pot, bring the stock (broth) to a boil. Reduce the heat to a simmer.

Generously season the short rib on both sides with salt and pepper. Place a large heavy skillet over high heat and add enough oil to lightly coat the surface. When the oil is piping hot, place the short rib in the skillet and cook, turning once, until deeply browned on both sides, about 3 minutes per side. Transfer the short rib to the simmering stock and cook, covered and over very low heat, until the short rib is very tender, about 2½ hours. Transfer to a plate and let rest until cool enough to handle. Reserve the stock for another use (or freeze up to 3 months).

Preheat the oven to 400°F (200°C/Gas Mark 6).

Place the rolls in the oven to warm and crisp while you finish preparing the short rib.

Trim and discard any large pieces of fat from the short rib, then slice it ¼ inch (.5 cm) thick. Place a large heavy skillet over high heat and add enough oil to lightly coat the surface. Once the oil is piping hot, add the sliced short rib and cook until the slices are browned on both sides, 1 to 2 minutes per side. Sprinkle lightly with salt and turn off the heat.

Cut the rolls almost, but not quite, all the way through and place them, cut side up, on a large work surface. In a small bowl, whisk together the mayonnaise and *sambal oelek* and evenly spread the mixture on the cut sides of the rolls.

Divide the meat, kimchee, and cilantro among the rolls. Close the sandwiches, cut each in half, and serve immediately.

NOTE: If you don't have Vietnamese Meat Stock (page 216), use an equal amount of high-quality store-bought beef stock and, along with the short rib, add 1 teaspoon each: kosher salt and sugar, 1 whole clove, 1 (1-inch/2.5 cm) cinnamon stick, ¼ star anise, 1 (1-inch/2.5 cm) piece roughly chopped fresh ginger, 1 (3 × 3-inch/7.5 × 7.5 cm) piece kombu, and 1 tablespoon fish sauce. Simmer for about 2½ hours, then strain the stock through a fine-mesh sieve. Reserve the meat and discard the remaining solids before proceeding with the rest of the recipe.

Ham, Gruyère, and Butter Lettuce Bánh Mì

MAKES 4 SANDWICHES

2 jalapeños, stemmed and thinly sliced
½ teaspoon kosher (coarse) salt
½ cup (120 ml) Mayonnaise (page 211)
   or high-quality store-bought
1 tablespoon *sambal oelek* chile paste
4 (6-inch/15 cm) Bánh Mì Rolls (page 166),
   high quality store-bought Vietnamese
   sandwich rolls, or Mexican *bolillos*
½ lb (230 g) thinly sliced high-quality
   French ham
4 oz (113 g) thinly sliced Gruyère cheese
Crispiest, innermost leaves of a head of
   butter lettuce (reserve the outer leaves
   for another use)
2 large handfuls cilantro (coriander) leaves

This decidedly atypical *bánh mì* is a nod to the French influence on our restaurant. We run it as a special whenever we accidentally order too much ham and Gruyère for our Ham and Cheese Croissants (page 176). Combining this familiar filling with cilantro (coriander), salted jalapeños, and spicy mayonnaise, you get a French sandwich seen through a Vietnamese lens and the result is excellent. If you can't get a hold of *bánh mì* rolls, French baguettes will do. Try to get lightly smoked ham and Gruyère on the younger, softer side.

Preheat the oven to 400°F (200°C/Gas Mark 6).

Place the jalapeños in a small bowl, sprinkle with the salt, toss to combine, and reserve. In another small bowl, whisk together the mayonnaise and *sambal oelek* and reserve.

Warm the rolls in the oven until the crusts are crisp and the insides are soft and warmed through, a couple of minutes. Cut the rolls lengthwise almost, but not quite, all the way through and place them, cut side up, on a large work surface. Evenly spread the *sambal oelek* mayonnaise on the cut sides of the rolls.

Evenly divide the ham, cheese, reserved sliced jalapeños, lettuce, and cilantro among the sandwiches. Close the sandwiches, cut each in half, and serve immediately.

Spicy Pork Meatball Bánh Mì with Quick-Pickled Carrots and Daikon

FOR THE PICKLES:

¼ cup (60 ml) unseasoned rice vinegar

2 tablespoons distilled white vinegar

2 tablespoons granulated sugar

½ teaspoon dried red chile flakes

2 teaspoons kosher (coarse) salt

1 large carrot, peeled and julienned

3 oz (85 g) daikon radish (½ medium radish), julienned

FOR THE MEATBALLS:

1 lb (455 g) coarsely ground pork

2 teaspoons kosher (coarse) salt

2 teaspoons packed dark brown sugar

½ teaspoon black pepper

1 teaspoon dried red chile flakes

1 scallion (spring onion), ends trimmed, minced

1 tablespoon minced fresh ginger

1 garlic clove, minced

½ teaspoon fish sauce

1 tablespoon canola (rapeseed) or vegetable oil

2 tablespoons tomato paste (purée)

2 tablespoons sambal oelek chile paste

FOR THE SANDWICHES:

½ cup (120 ml) Mayonnaise (page 211) or high-quality store-bought

1 tablespoon sambal oelek chile paste

4 (6-inch/15 cm) Bánh Mì Rolls (page 166), high-quality store-bought Vietnamese sandwich rolls, or Mexican bolillos

1 large handful cilantro (coriander) leaves

1 cucumber, thinly sliced

Essentially our meatball sub, this *bánh mì* came from the leftovers of other dishes on our menu. By combining meatballs from one of our *pho* dishes and the spicy, tomato broth from Bún Bo Hue (page 38) with all our *bánh mì* fixings, this was the result. This *bánh mì* pairs well with a cold beer.

MAKE THE PICKLES:

Place the vinegars, granulated sugar, chile flakes, and salt in a large bowl with ¼ cup (60 ml) water and whisk until the sugar is completely dissolved. Add the carrot and daikon and mix to combine. Let the vegetables marinate at room temperature while you prepare the meatballs.

MAKE THE MEATBALLS:

In a large bowl, combine the ground pork, salt, brown sugar, pepper, chile flakes, scallion, ginger, garlic, and fish sauce. Use your hands to thoroughly combine every-thing until the mixture is tacky. Form the mixture into 16 (1½-inch/4 cm) meatballs.

Set up a conventional steamer or a bamboo steamer inside of a large pot and fill the pot with water accordingly. Bring the water up to a boil. Put the meatballs into a shallow pan or dish that fits comfortably inside of the steamer and steam the meatballs, covered, until they are firm to the touch, about 15 minutes.

Meanwhile, heat the oil in a large heavy skillet, add the tomato paste and *sambal oelek*, and cook over medium heat, stirring, until the pastes are thoroughly fragrant and just barely beginning to brown, about 3 minutes. Use a slotted spoon or tongs to transfer the cooked meatballs to a plate and then carefully pour the liquid that has accumulated in the dish they cooked on into the tomato paste–*sambal oelek* mixture (2 pairs of tongs are helpful for carefully lifting the hot bowl out of the steamer). Whisk the cooking liquid into the pastes and bring the mixture to a boil. Reduce the heat and simmer, cooking the mixture until thick and glossy, about 3 minutes. Place the cooked meatballs in the mixture and gently stir to glaze the meatballs. Keep the meatballs warm over low heat while you assemble the sandwiches.

MAKE THE SANDWICHES:

Preheat the oven to 400°F (200°C/Mark 6).

In a small bowl, whisk together the mayonnaise and *sambal oelek* and reserve the mixture.

Warm the rolls in the oven until the crusts are crisp and the insides are soft and warmed through, a couple of minutes. Cut the rolls, lengthwise, almost, but not quite, all the way through and place them, cut side up, on a large work surface. Evenly spread the *sambal oelek* mayonnaise on the cut sides of the rolls.

Divide the glazed meatballs with some of their sauce evenly among the rolls. Drain the reserved carrot and daikon and divide them among the sandwiches along with the cilantro and cucumbers (discard the pickle brine or reserve it for another use, such as pickling more vegetables). Close the sandwiches, cut each in half, across, if you'd like, and serve immediately.

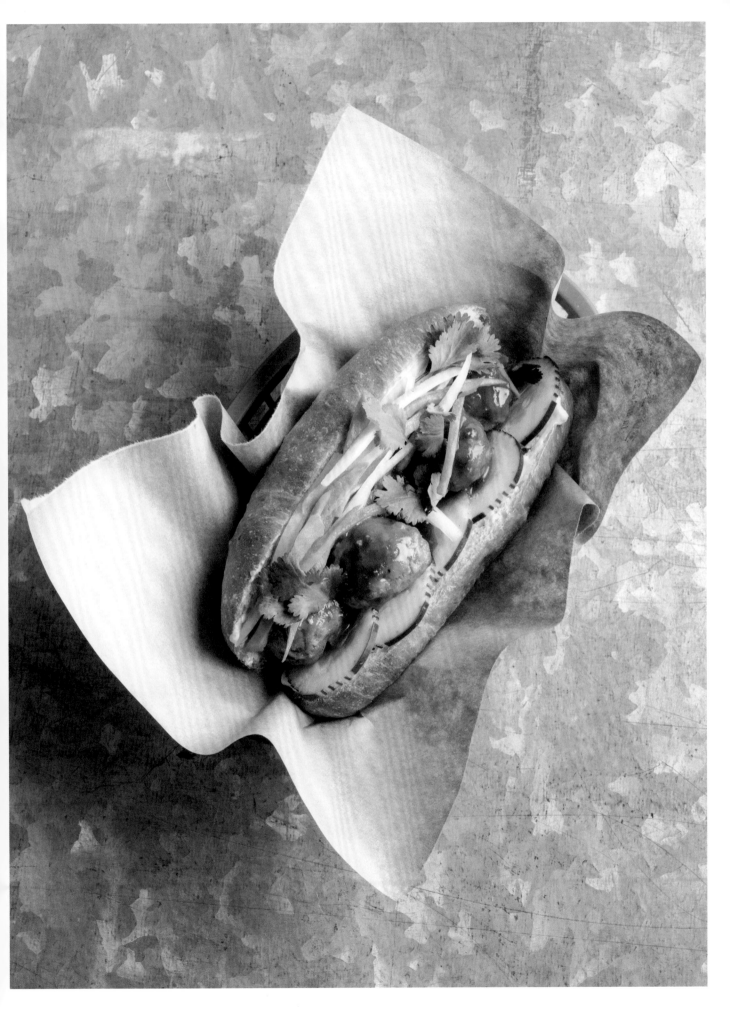

Classic Tam Deli Wonton Soup

SERVES 4

FOR THE WONTONS:

2 boneless, skinless chicken thighs
or ½ lb (230 g) coarsely ground dark
meat chicken

1 small garlic clove, minced

¼ teaspoon minced fresh lemongrass
(white part only)

¼ teaspoon kosher (coarse) salt

¼ teaspoon packed dark brown sugar

¼ teaspoon thinly sliced Thai bird chile
(about ½ chile)

2 scallions (spring onions), ends trimmed,
thinly sliced

¼ teaspoon fish sauce

1 large egg

12 fresh wonton wrappers (preferably
square)

FOR THE SOUP:

12 cups (3 liters) Vietnamese Meat Stock
made with chicken bones (page 216)

2 jalapeños, stemmed and thinly sliced

1 small handful cilantro (coriander) leaves,
roughly chopped

4 scallions (spring onions), ends trimmed,
thinly sliced

½ large white onion, thinly sliced

Elizabeth Street Café partly owes its existence to the influence and inspiration of the now-shuttered Tam Deli, a small Vietnamese restaurant in the northern part of Austin (one of our moms originally turned us onto it). The amazing sisters who ran it encouraged us to follow our vision and told us that the food that they make is their own spin on Vietnamese cooking. This idea of flexibility and adaptability gave us the feeling that we had freedom to do our own thing. This soup, also an homage to Tam Deli's, is one of our favorite soups to make and to eat.

MAKE THE WONTONS:

If using whole chicken thighs, trim off and discard any large pieces of fat or tendon. Cut the thighs into a very fine dice and place the meat in a large bowl with the garlic, lemongrass, salt, brown sugar, chile, scallions, and fish sauce. Mix well with a spoon until the chicken is tacky (you can also use a stand mixer fitted with a paddle attachment).

Crack the egg into a small bowl, whisk together with 2 tablespoons water, and reserve.

Lay out the wonton wrappers on a flat work surface. Wet your hands with water (to keep the chicken from sticking) and divide the chicken mixture into 12 equal portions. Put an equal portion of chicken in the center of each wonton wrapper. Forming the wontons one at a time, use a brush or your finger to apply the egg wash on the edges of each wrapper, then fold up the 4 corners to make a purse, pinching out as much air as possible. Pinch the seams together so they bind. Let the formed wontons sit for 2 minutes before cooking, so the egg wash seals the seams.

MAKE THE SOUP:

In a large pot, bring the stock (broth) to a boil. Add the wontons and cook for 1 minute, turning them with a spoon a few times so they cook evenly. Reduce the heat and simmer, covered, until the wonton wrappers are soft and the filling is cooked through, 2 more minutes. Uncover and stir in the jalapeño slices and cilantro. Ladle the soup, evenly distributing the wontons, into 4 bowls. Top each bowl with some of the scallions and white onion slices and serve immediately.

NOTE: If you don't have Vietnamese Meat Stock (page 216) on hand, use high-quality store-bought chicken stock and boost it with 2 whole cloves, 1 (2 × 2-inch/5 × 5 cm) cinnamon stick, 1 star anise, 1 (4-inch/10 cm) piece crushed fresh ginger, and 1 (8 × 8-inch/20 cm) piece dried kombu. Simmer the stock for about 25 minutes, then strain through a fine-mesh sieve (discard the solids). Finish with ¼ cup (60 ml) fish sauce and 2 teaspoons palm or granulated sugar. Season the stock to taste with salt and proceed with the rest of the recipe.

Spicy Vegetarian Pho

SERVES 4

1 recipe Vietnamese Vegetarian Stock
   (page 217)

Kosher (coarse) salt

1 oz (30 g) dried white tree or wood ear
   mushrooms

8 fresh shiitake mushrooms, stems
   discarded, roughly chopped

2 bunches (4 oz/115 g) fresh oyster
   mushrooms, tough stems discarded,
   roughly chopped

12 oz (340 g) firm tofu, cut into 1-inch
   (2.5 cm) cubes

⅓ cup (80 ml) *gochujang* chile paste, plus
   extra for serving

4 large handfuls baby spinach

14 oz (400 g) fresh *pho* noodles or ½ lb
   (230 g) dried

2 teaspoons toasted white sesame seeds

2 teaspoons ESC Fragrant Chile Oil (page
   206) or high-quality store-bought

2 teaspoons toasted sesame oil

½ small white onion, julienned

12 scallions (spring onions), ends trimmed,
   thinly sliced

Bean sprouts, Thai basil leaves, cilantro
   (coriander) leaves, thinly sliced radishes,
   and lime wedges, for serving

Bragg Liquid Aminos, for serving

Our vegetarian *pho* started out simple and has progressed to become more exciting and complex. At first it was just a clear vegetarian stock (broth), but then, we added *gochujang* chile paste and sesame oil and made sure our vegetarian stock could hold its own next to our not vegetarian ones. This *pho* went from a tame run-of-the-mill dish to a red and fiery version that borrows as much from Korean soup cooking as it does from Vietnamese *pho* traditions. We garnish the soup with fresh Thai basil and cilantro (coriander), which grow abundantly in our garden next door. Luckily, our central Texas climate is perfect for growing spicy herbs and piquant limes most of the year.

In a large pot over medium heat, bring the stock (broth) to a simmer. Bring a separate large pot of salted water to a boil.

    Meanwhile, put the dried mushrooms in a small bowl and cover with hot tap water. Place a plate over the mushrooms to keep them submerged. Soak until softened, about 10 minutes. Drain the mushrooms, discard the soaking liquid (or reserve it for another use, such as cooking grains), and discard the woody cores from the mushrooms. Roughly chop the mushrooms and add them to the simmering stock along with the fresh mushrooms and tofu. Cook until the mushrooms are softened, about 2 minutes.

    Place the *gochujang* in a small bowl and add 1 large ladle of the warm stock. Whisk together, then return the mixture to the stock and stir well to combine. Add the spinach to the soup and cook just until wilted, about 1 minute. Season the stock to taste with salt.

    Cook the noodles in the pot with the salted boiling water until they have just softened but still have a bit of bite (either 2 minutes for fresh or up to 6 for dried). Drain the noodles in a colander. Warm 4 large soup bowls in a 300°F (150°C/ Gas Mark 2) oven for 1 minute or in the microwave for 30 seconds. Evenly divide the noodles between the bowls.

    Ladle the soup over the noodles and evenly distribute the vegetables and tofu among the bowls. Divide the sesame seeds, chile oil, sesame oil, julienned onion, and scallions among the bowls. Serve immediately with a platter full of bean sprouts, Thai basil, cilantro, sliced radishes, and lime wedges to add to your soups as you like. Have a bottle of Bragg Liquid Aminos and some *gochujang* on hand to stir into your soup.

Sticky Rice Bowls with Pork, Bok Choy, and Hon Shimeji

SERVES 4

FOR THE PORK:

¾ lb (340 g) boneless pork shoulder
   (ask your butcher for a single thinly
   sliced piece)

2 tablespoons fish sauce

2 tablespoons sugar

1 scallion (spring onion), ends trimmed,
   thinly sliced

FOR THE BOWLS:

Kosher (coarse) salt

4 eggs

2 tablespoons canola (rapeseed)
   or vegetable oil

2 garlic cloves, thinly sliced

1 Fresno or other fresh red chile, stemmed
   and thinly sliced

1 bunch *hon shimeji* mushrooms, stems
   discarded

2 bunches baby bok choy, leaves roughly
   chopped and cores discarded

1 teaspoon fish sauce

Juice of ½ lemon

2 scallions (spring onions), ends trimmed,
   thinly sliced

Cooked sticky rice (page 22 from Sicky
   Rice with Ginger Sausage, Herb Salad,
   and Poached Eggs)

3 tablespoons hoisin sauce

2 teaspoons fresh lime juice

2 teaspoons unseasoned rice vinegar

1½ tablespoons sriracha

Extra-virgin olive oil, for drizzling

Fleur de sel, for serving

Seto fumi furikake or toasted sesame
   seeds, for serving

1 large handful cilantro (coriander) leaves,
   Thai basil leaves, or a combination,
   for garnish

If you can't find *hon shimeji* (or beech) mushrooms, try a mix of fresh shiitake and oyster mushrooms. The eggs can be cooked ahead, peeled, kept covered in cold water, and reheated before serving.

MAKE THE PORK:

Place the pork between 2 large pieces of plastic wrap (clingfilm). Using a mallet or a heavy ramekin, gently pound the pork to tenderize and flatten it to ¼ inch (6 mm) thick.

In a small bowl, whisk together the fish sauce, sugar, scallion, and 2 tablespoons water until the sugar dissolves. Pour the marinade into a large resealable plastic bag, add the pork, and squeeze all the air out of the bag so that the marinade completely covers the meat. Refrigerate for at least 4 hours and up to overnight.

Heat a grill or a grill (griddle) pan with high heat. Remove the pork from the marinade, brush off the scallions, and pat the meat dry with paper towels. Reduce the heat to medium-low and grill the pork until charred on both sides and firm to the touch, 2 to 3 minutes per side. Transfer the pork to a cutting (chopping) board and set aside.

ASSEMBLE THE BOWLS:

Bring a medium pot of generously salted water to a boil (the salt will make the eggs easier to peel). Fill a large bowl with ice water. Add the eggs to the boiling water, and cook the eggs for exactly 6 minutes. Immediately transfer the eggs to the ice bath for 1 minute, then peel while the eggs are still a little warm. Set aside.

In a large skillet set over high heat, warm the canola oil, then add the garlic, chile, mushrooms, and bok choy, and cook, stirring, until the vegetables are just softened, about 4 minutes. Season with the fish sauce and lemon juice, taste, and adjust seasoning if needed. Season to taste with salt. Stir in the scallions and reserve.

Warm 4 bowls in a 300°F (150°C/Gas Mark 2) oven for 1 minute or in the microwave for 30 seconds. Distribute the rice among the bowls. In a small bowl, whisk together the hoisin, lime juice, vinegar, and sriracha. Spoon the sauce over the rice. Thinly slice the reserved pork and divide it—and the vegetables—among the bowls. Make an indentation in each bowl to hold an egg and place 1 egg in each bowl. Drizzle each egg with about a teaspoon of olive oil, and sprinkle with a pinch of fleur de sel and a generous shake of the *furikake*. Garnish each bowl with herbs and serve immediately.

Chilled Dipping Noodles with Crab, Scallion, Bonito, and Black Vinegar

SERVES 4

¾ cup (180 ml) Chinese black vinegar

2 tablespoons white shoyu or 1 tablespoon soy sauce

4 teaspoons Chinese chile oil, divided

Kosher (coarse) salt

6 scallions (spring onions), ends trimmed, thinly sliced into matchsticks

2 celery stalks, shaved

14 oz (400 g) fresh Korean *udon jjajang* noodles

6 oz (170 g) high-quality fresh crabmeat, picked over for shells and cartilage

Fleur de sel and black pepper

1 small handful store-bought crispy fried shallots

1 small handful bonito flakes

We love chilled noodles, especially when it's hot outside or we feel like eating something light. We use fresh Korean *udon jjajang* noodles for this, which are thinner and chewier than Japanese-style *udon* noodles and sometimes called "knife-cut" vermicelli. The black vinegar and bonito deepen the flavor, while the crisp scallions (spring onions) and celery offer up refreshing texture. For the chile oil, we prefer the Lao Gan Ma brand, also known as Old Godmother—the label has a photo of an elderly woman.

Mix together the vinegar, shoyu, and 2 teaspoons of the chile oil. Divide the mixture among 4 small bowls and reserve.

Bring a large pot of lightly salted water to a boil.

Meanwhile, place the scallions and celery in a large bowl of ice water and let them sit until they curl, about 10 minutes. Transfer the vegetables to a paper towel to drain and reserve the ice water.

Cook the noodles in the boiling water until they're just cooked through, about 3 minutes. Drain the noodles in a colander, then transfer to the reserved ice-water bath to chill completely. Once cool, drain again.

Place the cooled, drained noodles into a large bowl and add the remaining 2 teaspoons chile oil sauce and the crab. Stir to combine. Divide the noodles among 4 bowls. Season each portion with a pinch of fleur de sel and a few grinds of pepper. Top each bowl evenly with the scallions, celery, shallots, and bonito flakes. Serve immediately with the reserved vinegar sauce alongside for dipping.

DINNER

BE TH
BÁNH MÌ
ugerie

Akaushi Carpaccio with Shishito Peppers and Marinated Mushrooms

SERVES 4

1 lb (455 g) high-quality eye of round beef
  or beef tenderloin
2 tablespoons canola (rapeseed)
  or vegetable oil
About 20 (90 g/3 oz) shishito peppers
Kosher (coarse) salt and black pepper
2½ tablespoons fresh lemon juice
1½ tablespoons soy sauce
1 batch Marinated Hon Shimeji Mushrooms
  (page 212), drained
1 large handful cilantro (coriander) leaves,
  finely chopped
1 large handful fresh watercress leaves

Bò tái chanh is Vietnam's answer to carpaccio: thinly sliced beef that, like ceviche, is "cooked" with lime or lemon juice. We like ours with lots of lemon and assemble this right before we're ready to eat, since the acid cooks the meat quickly. We like to use Japanese akaushi beef, because it is well marbled; kobe or wagyu also work well. If you can't find eye of round steak, substitute beef tenderloin or the highest-quality meat you can find.

Wrap the beef tightly in plastic wrap (clingfilm) and twist the edges like a candy wrappers, to form the beef into a tight cylinder. Freeze the beef for 30 minutes (this will make it easier to slice).

Meanwhile, heat the oil in a large skillet and, when piping hot, add the peppers and cook over high heat, stirring now and then, until the peppers are softened and charred in spots, about 3 minutes. Season the peppers generously with salt, transfer them to a plate, and reserve.

Remove the meat from the freezer, unwrap it, and slice it as thinly as possible. Divide the meat among 4 (10-inch/25 cm) round plates, shingling the pieces so they cover the plate in an even layer. If any of the pieces are uneven or too thick, cover with plastic wrap and pound with a mallet or a small heavy-bottomed pot. Season each plate of meat generously with pepper.

Mix together the lemon juice and soy sauce in a small bowl, then drizzle the mixture evenly among the plates. Tilt each plate to cover the beef with the marinade (it should touch every bit of the meat, but the meat shouldn't swim in the liquid). Divide the mushrooms among the plates and scatter the cilantro over each dish. Divide the reserved shishitos among the dishes and top each with some of the watercress. Serve immediately.

Ginger-Chile Oil Dumplings

SERVES 4

FOR THE SAUCE:

½ cup (120 ml) Vietnamese Meat Stock
   (page 216)

1 tablespoon finely chopped cilantro
   (coriander) leaves

1 small garlic clove, minced

2 teaspoons white shoyu or 1 teaspoon
   soy sauce

1 teaspoon soy sauce

½ teaspoon minced fresh ginger

½ teaspoon thinly sliced fresh Thai bird
   chile (about 1 chile)

½ teaspoon fish sauce

½ teaspoon fresh lime juice or unseasoned
   rice vinegar

FOR THE DUMPLINGS:

6 oz (170 g) ground pork

6 oz (170 g) shrimp (prawns), peeled,
   deveined, and finely chopped

1 (8 oz/230 g) can water chestnuts,
   drained, rinsed, and diced small

1 teaspoon kosher (coarse) salt

½ teaspoon fish sauce

¼ teaspoon sugar

1 garlic clove, minced

1 scallion (spring onion), ends trimmed,
   minced

Pinch of minced fresh lemongrass (white
   part only; optional)

1 fresh Thai bird chile, thinly sliced

32 fresh wonton wrappers (preferably
   square)

TO SERVE:

¼ cup (60 ml) ESC Fragrant Chile Oil (page
   206) or high-quality store-bought, for
   serving

3 scallions (spring onions), ends trimmed,
   thinly sliced

1 serrano or other fresh chile, stemmed and
   thinly sliced

Cilantro (coriander) and watercress leaves,
   for serving

1 large handful store-bought crispy fried
   shallots

1 lemon, quartered into wedges

These dumplings, one of our bestsellers, are a perfect example of the Chinese-style dishes that have found a home on our menu. They also speak to the versatility of an Asian pantry: once you have ingredients like soy sauce, fresh ginger, and chile, you can go in many directions. They are not only staples for many of our Vietnamese recipes, but they're also some of the key flavors behind Chinese, Japanese, and Korean dishes. Realizing how widely used these ingredients are is a nice reminder of how great it can be to combine influences from different cultures in one dish. The Vietnamese garnish of cilantro (coriander), fried shallots, and fresh lemon on these Chinese-inspired dumplings is a perfect example.

MAKE THE SAUCE:
Whisk the stock (broth), cilantro, garlic, white shoyu, soy sauce, ginger, chile, fish sauce, and lime juice in a bowl and set aside.

MAKE THE DUMPLINGS:
In a large bowl set over an even larger bowl of ice, combine the pork, shrimp, water chestnuts, salt, fish sauce, sugar, garlic, scallion, lemongrass (if using), and chile. Use a spoon or your hands to thoroughly mix together.

   Fill a small bowl with water and set aside. Lay out 8 of the wonton wrappers on a flat work surface. Wet your hands with water and put a heaping teaspoon size of the filling in the center of each wrapper (wetting your hands will help keep the filling from sticking to them). Forming the wontons one at a time, use a brush or your finger to moisten the edges of each wrapper with water and then fold up all 4 corners to make a purse, pinching out as much air as possible. Pinch the seams together so that they bind. Let the formed wontons sit for 2 minutes before cooking so that the water seals the seams. Repeat the process with the remaining wrappers and filling.

TO SERVE:
Bring a large pot of water to a boil and add the dumplings. Boil the dumplings until the skins are just about translucent and all the wontons float to the top of the pot, 4 to 5 minutes. Use a large slotted spoon or a spider to transfer the dumplings to a large nonstick skillet set over high heat. Add the reserved sauce, bring to a boil, and gently toss to coat the dumplings with the sauce. Evenly divide the dumplings among 4 shallow bowls and drizzle each portion with some of the chile oil. Top each with some of the scallions, serrano, cilantro, watercress, and crispy fried shallots. Squeeze a lemon wedge over the dumplings and serve immediately.

   NOTE: If you don't have Vietnamese Meat Stock (page 216), use high-quality store-bought beef stock and add an additional splash of fish sauce.

Steamed Oysters with Nuoc Cham, XO Sauce, and Crispy Garlic

SERVES 4

24 garlic cloves, peeled and thinly sliced, or store-bought garlic chips or shallots

2 cups (475 ml) canola (rapeseed) or vegetable oil

Kosher (coarse) salt (optional)

2 tablespoons Nuoc Cham (page 208)

2 tablespoons fresh lime juice

1 tablespoon ESC XO Sauce (page 208)

½ teaspoon finely grated or minced fresh lemongrass (white part only)

12 fresh oysters

1 scallion (spring onion), very thinly sliced

Lime slice, dipped partially in *gochugaru* (Korean chile powder, for garnish (optional)

These oysters were inspired by a recipe in *The Art of Living According to Joe Beef,* the cookbook from Joe Beef restaurant in Montreal. Steaming oysters is a great way to prepare them at home, because shucking the oysters becomes much easier once they are cooked. At the restaurant, we prefer a creamy West Coast (of North America) oyster like Pacific Orchard or Komo Gway—but use whatever quality oysters you can find and, if you don't have an oyster platter, serve them on a bed of salt.

Put the garlic in a small pot and cover with cold water. Bring to a boil, strain the garlic in a sieve and return the garlic to the pot. Cover it once again with fresh cold water and repeat the process 2 more times. Dry the blanched garlic on paper towels.

Line a small bowl with paper towels. Heat the oil in a medium pot, add the blanched, dried garlic, and fry over medium-high heat, stirring continuously, until the garlic is light golden brown, about 2 minutes. Regulate the heat as you fry, turning it down if the garlic is browning too quickly, or turning it up if it isn't sizzling. Use a slotted spoon or a spider to transfer the garlic to the lined bowl. Season the garlic chips with salt and set aside.

If you don't have an oyster serving platter, fill a serving platter with a thick layer of salt.

Place the *nuoc cham*, lime juice, XO sauce, and lemongrass in another small bowl and whisk together. Transfer the mixture to a small pitcher (a liquid measuring cup [jug] works well) and reserve.

Set up a conventional steamer or a bamboo steamer inside of a large pot and fill the pot with water accordingly. Bring the water to a boil. Arrange the oysters, rounded shell sides down, in the steamer and scrunch up a few pieces of aluminum foil to bolster the oysters as needed so that they don't tip. Steam the oysters until the top shells are slightly open and the oysters are heated through, 3 to 4 minutes. Using tongs, remove and discard the top shells from the oysters and then transfer the oysters to the prepared serving platter (the salt will keep them from tipping). Use an oyster knife or a paring knife to make sure each oyster is loosened from its bottom shell. Divide the reserved *nuoc cham* mixture between the oysters. Cover each oyster with some garlic chips and sprinkle scallion over the oysters. Serve immediately.

NOTE: If you don't have *nuoc cham* on hand, mix together 1 tablespoon fish sauce, 1 tablespoon of water, and a pinch of sugar for a substitute.

Escargots with Thai Basil-Curry Butter

SERVES 3

FOR THE BUTTER:

¼ lb (115 g) butter, at room temperature

2 large or 3 small shallots, minced

1 large handful Thai basil leaves, minced

1½ tablespoons yellow curry paste

Finely grated zest of 1 lemon (reserve
   the zested lemon for serving)

½ teaspoon kosher (coarse) salt

FOR THE HERB SALAD:

1 small handful tarragon leaves

1 large handful Thai basil leaves

1 large handful mint leaves

1 large handful parsley leaves

1 tablespoon fresh lemon juice

2 tablespoons extra-virgin olive oil

Kosher (coarse) salt and black pepper

TO SERVE:

1 (7 oz/200 g) can extra-large escargots,
   drained and rinsed (18 escargots)

1 Classic French Baguette (page 164) or
   high-quality store-bought, cut into thirds

This dish is as much about the snails as it is about our homemade baguettes—truly a great excuse for eating lots of bread dipped in delicious butter. Because most cans of escargots have eighteen snails and most escargots serving dishes have six spots, we designed this recipe to work for three people. If you don't have escargots serving dishes, you can cook the snails in a small baking dish.

MAKE THE BUTTER:
Place the butter, shallots, Thai basil, curry paste, lemon zest, and salt in a large bowl and whisk until combined. Reserve the compound butter.

MAKE THE HERB SALAD:
Put the tarragon, Thai basil, mint, and parsley into a large bowl and drizzle over the lemon juice and oil. Use your hands to mix the herbs together and season the salad to taste with salt and pepper. Reserve the salad.

TO SERVE:
Preheat the broiler to high.
   Divide the escargots among 3 broiler-safe escargot dishes (each dish typically has 6 spaces). Spread each escargot with plenty of the reserved butter, dividing it evenly among all the escargots and mounding it on top of each escargot. Place the dishes on a sheet pan and transfer the sheet pan to the broiler. Broil the escargots, rotating the tray as needed so they cook evenly, until the butter begins to brown, about 5 minutes. (Depending on the strength of your broiler, the snails might use more or less time, so keep an eye on them.) Carefully place the baguettes in the bottom of the hot oven to warm while the escargots cook. Transfer the escargots dishes to large plates and place a piece of baguette alongside each one. Cut the reserved lemon into wedges and divide among the plates along with herb salad on the side. Serve immediately.

Char-Grilled Flank Steak Spring Rolls

MAKES 12 ROLLS

2 tablespoons fish sauce

2 tablespoons sugar

½ lb (230 g) flank stank

3 scallions (spring onions), ends trimmed, thinly sliced

2 tablespoons extra-virgin olive oil

Black pepper

2 oz (60 g) rice vermicelli

12 rice papers

1 English cucumber, thinly sliced

1 jalapeño, stemmed and thinly sliced

2 large handfuls cilantro (coriander) leaves

1 small head red leaf lettuce (about 2 large handfuls), thinly sliced

Nuoc Cham (page 208), Sweet Chile Vinegar (page 208), or Peanut Sauce (page 206), for dipping

Spring rolls are best when served them shortly after being made. Here, marinated flank steak takes the spotlight. You can grill (griddle) the steak and prepare the rest of the fillings ahead of time, then assemble the rolls right before you eat. These spring rolls are a fun DIY activity with friends or kids.

In a medium bowl, whisk together the fish sauce and sugar with 2 tablespoons water until the sugar has dissolved. Pour the mixture into a large resealable plastic bag and add the steak and the scallions. Squeeze all the air out of the bag so the marinade is completely covering the steak. Refrigerate and let the steak marinate for at least 3 hours and up to overnight.

Heat a grill or grill (griddle) pan to very high heat. Remove the steak from the marinade and brush off the scallions. Pat the steak dry with paper towels. Transfer the steak to a plate (or another clean surface), drizzle both sides with the oil, and season both sides with pepper. Grill the steak until nicely charred on both sides but still quite soft to the touch and rare in the middle, 2 to 3 minutes per side. (If you prefer it more well done, cook for a few extra minutes on each side.) Transfer the steak to a clean plate and let cool to room temperature. Cover the steak with plastic wrap (clingfilm) and refrigerate until very cold, at least 3 hours.

Bring a medium pot of water to a boil and cook the rice noodles for exactly 4 minutes, stirring gently to separate them. Drain the noodles in a colander and rinse with cool water to wash off the extra starch. Let the noodles sit for 15 minutes so the excess water drains and the noodles come to room temperature—they should be a little sticky.

While the noodles cool, slice the cold steak against the grain into thin strips. Gather the rest of the filling ingredients so you are ready to wrap.

Fill a large bowl with room temperature water next to a clean work surface. Working with 1 piece of rice paper at a time, quickly dip the rice paper in the water until it just starts to soften, about 10 seconds. The rice paper will continue to soften as you make the roll. Pat the paper dry on both sides with a clean cotton dish towel. Shingle 3 cucumber slices on the softened rice paper, followed by some of the noodles and 3 strips of steak alongside the cucumber. Top with some jalapeño, cilantro, and a small pile of lettuce. Wrap the springroll up tightly as if it were a small burrito. Repeat the process with the remaining wrappers and fillings. Serve immediately with *nuoc cham*, chile vinegar, and/or peanut sauce for dipping.

Singapore Noodles with Gulf Shrimp and Roasted Pork

SERVES 4

This is the first dish we put on the menu at ESC. It remains one of our best sellers and is a hit not only with Tom's daughter, who consumes these noodles by the handful, but also with Dustin Keller, a former football player with the New York Jets, who orders a double serving five times a week for breakfast. Inspired by Dustin, we put these noodles on our breakfast menu without the shrimp (prawns) and serve them with sunny-side-up eggs on top.

FOR THE PORK:

¼ cup (60 ml) canola (rapeseed) or vegetable oil

2 tablespoons annatto seeds

1 lb (455 g) boneless pork shoulder (also called pork butt—ask the butcher for an even, square piece)

1 teaspoon sugar

1 teaspoon kosher (coarse) salt

FOR THE CURRY SLURRY:

1 tablespoon Madras curry powder

¾ teaspoon ground turmeric

2 teaspoons fish sauce

½ teaspoon sriracha

½ teaspoon minced fresh ginger

FOR THE NOODLES:

½ lb (230 g) rice vermicelli

¼ cup (60 ml) canola (rapeseed) or vegetable oil

½ large white onion, julienned

1 jalapeño, stemmed and thinly sliced, or more to taste

1 Fresno or other fresh red chile, stemmed and thinly sliced

12 medium gulf shrimp (prawns), about ½ lb (230 g), peeled and deveined

2 eggs

2 large handfuls cilantro (coriander) leaves

6 scallions (spring onions), ends trimmed, thinly sliced

1 large handful watercress (the thicker the stems, the better)

1 lime, cut into wedges

Sriracha, for serving

MAKE THE PORK:

In a small pot set over low heat, warm the oil, add the annatto seeds, and cook, stirring twice, until the seeds are fragrant and sizzling and the oil is brick red, about 5 minutes. Strain the oil through a sieve into a small bowl and discard the seeds. Cool the oil to room temperature.

Season the pork all over with the sugar and the salt. Put the pork in a large resealable plastic bag and pour in the annatto oil. Squeeze all the air out of the bag so the oil completely covers the pork. Refrigerate and let marinate for at least 4 hours and up to overnight.

Preheat the oven to 350°F (175°C/Gas Mark 4).

Set a roasting rack or metal wire rack over a sheet pan. Put the pork on the rack and drizzle whatever oil remains in the bag over the pork (it's okay if it drips into the pan). Roast until the pork is browned and tender, about 2½ hours, turning it halfway through roasting. Remove the pork from the oven and let cool to room temperature; then cut into large bite-size pieces—discarding any large pieces of fat—and reserve. Reserve the bright red fat in the sheet pan.

MAKE THE CURRY SLURRY:

In a small bowl, whisk together the curry powder, turmeric, fish sauce, sriracha, and ginger with ¼ cup (60 ml) water. Let sit for 1 hour at room temperature. Cover and refrigerate for up to 3 days.

MAKE THE NOODLES:

Line a plate with a clean cotton dish towel. Put the noodles in a large bowl of hot tap water and soak until softened, about 5 minutes. Drain the noodles and transfer to the lined plate. Place a second clean cotton dish towel on top of the noodles, cover with plastic wrap (clingfilm), and refrigerate for up to 2 days.

In a large wok or seasoned carbon-steel fry pan set over high heat warm the oil until smoking. (If your pan is small, cook the noodles in 2 batches.) Then add the reserved pork, and cook until the meat is crisp on one side, about 3 minutes. Add the onion, jalapeño, and Fresno chile and cook, stirring, until the vegetables pick up some color, about 5 minutes. Add the shrimp and cook until browned on both sides, 1 to 2 minutes per side. Add the reserved pork fat from the roasting pan and the noodles and stir rapidly to combine the ingredients in the pan. Move the stir-fry to one side of the pan and crack the eggs into the pan, stirring with a wooden spoon or chopsticks scramble the eggs and to incorporate them into the noodles. Then stir the curry slurry and pour it over the noodles. Continue to stir and toss the noodles to evenly distribute the slurry. Stir in most of the cilantro and scallions and taste for seasoning, adding more salt if needed.

Transfer the stir-fry to a serving platter, and place some of the shrimp on top of the noodles. Top with the remaining cilantro and scallions and the watercress. Serve immediately with the lime wedges and sriracha.

Manila Clam and Ginger Fried Rice

SERVES 4

2 tablespoons sriracha

2 tablespoons unseasoned rice vinegar

2 tablespoons fish sauce

¼ cup (60 ml) canola (rapeseed) or
vegetable oil, plus extra if needed

1 yellow onion, finely diced

1 jalapeño, stemmed and minced

Kosher (coarse) salt and black pepper

4 cups (600 g) cold cooked long-grain
white rice (leftover take-out [take-away]
rice is perfect for this)

2 eggs

1 cup (100 g) fresh mung bean sprouts

2 large handfuls shredded napa cabbage

1 large handful cilantro (coriander) leaves,
roughly chopped

1 large handful Thai basil leaves, roughly
chopped

2 scallions (spring onions), ends trimmed,
thinly sliced, plus extra for serving

1 (2-inch/5 cm) piece fresh ginger, cut
into the thinnest matchsticks possible,
divided

24 Manila clams, scrubbed

2 tablespoons extra-virgin olive oil

½ lemon, for serving

Like the "Shaking Beef" recipe that evolved into the Grilled Rib-Eye Fried Rice (page 108), this fried rice started as a classic Chinese dish of clams with black bean sauce. Clams are a hard sell in Texas since they're not common here, and combining them with fermented black beans—another uncommon ingredient—didn't help the cause. However, we love clams and wanted to keep them on the menu, so we added them to familiar fried rice and people went crazy for this dish. If you can't find Manila clams, cockles make a great substitute.

In a small bowl, whisk together the sriracha, vinegar, and fish sauce. Reserve the sauce.

Heat the canola oil in a large nonstick skillet and, when piping hot, add the onion and jalapeño, and season with a big pinch of salt and a few grinds of black pepper. Cook over high heat, stirring now and then, until the vegetables begin to soften and just barely begin to brown, about 5 minutes. Use your hands to crumble in the rice; if it seems dry, add up to 2 tablespoons more oil. Cook the rice, stirring to break up any clumps, until it's nice and hot, about 5 minutes. Move the rice to the edges of the pan and crack the eggs directly in the center of the pan. Stir the eggs to combine the whites and the yolks and to cook them through and then stir them into the rice. Add the bean sprouts, cabbage, and reserved sriracha mixture and stir to combine the ingredients with the rice. Stir in the cilantro, basil, scallions, and half of the ginger. Season the rice to taste with salt and keep warm over low heat.

Meanwhile, set up a conventional or a bamboo steamer inside of a large pot and fill the pot with water accordingly. Bring the water to a boil. Put the clams into a shallow pan or dish that fits comfortably inside of the steamer. Cover and steam just until the clams open, about 2 minutes. Discard any that do not open and be sure to reserve the liquid that has collected in the dish.

Carefully stir half of the cooked clams into the rice, shells and all, and then transfer the rice to a large serving platter. Top with the remaining clams and spoon the liquid that the clams released over the rice (no need to use every last bit of it and definitely leave any grit in the dish and not on the rice). Drizzle the exposed clams with the olive oil. Sprinkle the remaining ginger and a bit of extra scallions on top and serve immediately with lemon on the side.

Bánh Cuôn with Twice-Cooked Pork and Herb Salad

SERVES 4

FOR THE FILLING:

⅓ oz (20 g) dried wood ear mushrooms

½ lb (230 g) boneless pork shoulder (ask your butcher for a single thinly sliced piece)

1 teaspoon kosher (coarse) salt

3 teaspoons sugar, divided

2 tablespoons fish sauce, divided

2 tablespoons canola (rapeseed) or vegetable oil

1 small yellow onion, thinly sliced

1 heaping tablespoon sriracha

FOR THE SALAD:

1 small dried *chile de árbol*, finely chopped

½ small shallot, minced

¼ cup (60 ml) unseasoned rice vinegar

1 tablespoon canola (rapeseed) or vegetable oil

1 large handful each Thai basil leaves, mint leaves, and cilantro (coriander) leaves

1 cup (100 g) fresh mung bean sprouts

FOR THE BÁNH CUÔN:

⅓ cup plus 1 teaspoon (40 g) nonglutinous white rice flour

⅓ cup plus 1 teaspoon (40 g) glutinous rice flour

⅔ cup plus 2 teaspoons (80 g) tapioca starch

Pinch of kosher (coarse) salt

Cooking spray

TO SERVE:

2 tablespoons fish sauce

2 tablespoons extra-virgin olive oil

1 large handful store-bought crispy fried shallots, for garnish

1 cup (240 ml) Nuoc Cham (page 208), for serving

Bánh cuôn are large flat noodles made from rice and tapioca flours that get filled, rolled, and then cut into bite-size pieces. A popular street-food snack, the noodle batter is steamed on a cotton cloth stretched over a pot of water. Notoriously difficult to make, we studied every recipe and video we could find—and made hundreds of batches, varying types of rice flour and ratios, before landing on the recipe below. While using a nonstick pan is unorthodox, it's a sure way to make successful *bánh cuôn* at home. The pork and wood ear mushroom filling is traditional, but feel free to fill *bánh cuôn* with whatever you like—they're great with shrimp (prawns).

MAKE THE FILLING:

In a large bowl, cover the mushrooms with hot tap water and weigh down with a plate. Soak until softened, about 20 minutes. Drain the mushrooms (discard the soaking liquid), then thinly slice them and reserve.

Meanwhile, place the pork between 2 large pieces of thin plastic wrap (clingfilm). Using a mallet or small heavy-bottomed pot, gently pound the pork to about ¼ inch (6 mm) thick. Sprinkle the pork on both sides with the salt and 1 teaspoon of the sugar and rub the salt and sugar into the meat.

Heat a grill or a grill (griddle) pan to medium heat. Grill the pork, brushing it while it cooks with 1 tablespoon of the fish sauce, until charred on both sides and firm to the touch, 2 to 3 minutes per side. Transfer the pork to a cutting (chopping) board and let cool.

Thinly slice the rested pork, discarding any large pieces of fat or sinew.

In a large skillet set over high heat, warm the oil until piping hot. Add the sliced pork and cook, stirring, until the pork is crispy on the edges, about 3 minutes. Add the onion and cook, stirring, until the onion starts to soften and just barely pick up color, about 5 minutes. Stir in the reserved mushrooms and cook for 1 minute. Add the remaining 2 teaspoons sugar, the remaining 1 tablespoon fish sauce, and the sriracha and cook just until the liquid evaporates, about 1 minute. Turn off the heat and set aside.

MAKE THE SALAD:

In a small bowl, whisk together the *chile de árbol*, shallot, vinegar, and oil; set aside.

Right before serving, in a small bowl, dress the herbs and bean sprouts with the *chile de árbol* dressing and toss to combine.

MAKE THE BÁNH CUÔN:

In a large bowl, whisk together both flours, the tapioca starch, and the salt. Whisk in ¾ cup (180 ml) cold water until the batter is smooth.

Lightly coat with cooking spray a 10-inch (25 cm) nonstick pan and set over medium heat. Add a quarter of the noodle batter, swirling the pan to evenly and thinly coat the bottom. Cover the pan and cook the batter until the edges are a little transparent and the center is bright white, 2 to 3 minutes. Uncover the pan, drizzle 1 to 2 teaspoons of water over the *bánh cuôn*, re-cover, and cook for about 1 minute, until the *bánh cuôn* is cooked through and translucent. Add a quarter of the pork filling to one side of the *bánh cuôn* and roll the *bánh cuôn* over the filling. Carefully transfer the *bánh cuôn* to an oval plate and use a pair of scissors to cut it into 5 pieces. Repeat the process 3 more times.

TO SERVE:

Drizzle the fish sauce and olive oil over each *bánh cuôn*. Divide the herb salad among the plates and then garnish each *bánh cuôn* with the crispy fried shallots. Divide the *nuoc cham* among 4 small bowls and place one alongside each plate. Serve immediately.

Grilled Rib-Eye Fried Rice

SERVES 4

⅓ oz (20 g) dried wood ear mushrooms

2 tablespoons sriracha

2 tablespoons unseasoned rice vinegar

2 tablespoons fish sauce

1 (12 oz/340 g) rib-eye steak

Kosher (coarse) salt and black pepper

¼ cup (60 ml) canola (rapeseed) or
  vegetable oil, plus extra if needed

1 yellow onion, finely diced

1 jalapeño, stemmed and minced

1 Fresno or other fresh red chile, stemmed
  and minced

4 cups (600 g) cold cooked long-grain
  white rice (leftover take-out [take-away]
  rice is perfect for this)

2 eggs

1 cup (100 g) fresh mung bean sprouts

2 large handfuls shredded napa cabbage

1 large handful fresh cilantro (coriander)
  leaves, roughly chopped, plus a little
  extra for serving

2 scallions (spring onions), ends trimmed,
  thinly sliced

3 tablespoons Fish Sauce Caramel
  (page 212)

Small handful bonito flakes (optional)

We used to have a dish called "Shaking Beef," a simple beef and onion stir-fry, but its popularity with our patrons was lackluster, so we started mixing the beef with rice for our restaurant family meal. It was good, but we tweaked the dish yet again, into fried rice with sliced rib eye on top. The bonito flake garnish adds a salty hit and also makes for an unusual presentation, since the thin flakes "dance" when they hit the hot rice.

In a large bowl, cover the mushrooms with hot tap water and weigh down with a plate. Soak until softened, about 20 minutes. Drain the mushrooms (discard the soaking liquid), then thinly slice them and reserve.

In a small bowl, whisk together the sriracha, vinegar, and fish sauce. Reserve the sauce.

Heat a grill or a grill (griddle) pan to medium heat. Season the steak aggressively on both sides with salt and pepper and grill until charred on both sides and just barely firm to the touch, 2 to 3 minutes per side. Transfer the steak to a cutting (chopping) board and let it rest while you prepare the fried rice.

Heat the oil in a large nonstick skillet and, when piping hot, add the onion, jalapeño, Fresno chile, and the reserved wood ear mushrooms, and season with a big pinch of salt and a few grinds of pepper. Cook over high heat, stirring now and then, until the vegetables begin to soften and just barely begin to brown, about 5 minutes. Use your hands to crumble in the rice; if it seems dry, add up to 2 more tablespoons oil. Cook the rice, stirring to break up any clumps, until hot, about 5 minutes. Move the rice to the edges of the pan and crack the eggs directly in the center of the pan. Stir the eggs to combine the whites and the yolks and to cook them through and then stir them into the rice. Add the bean sprouts and the cabbage and stir to combine them with the rice. Stir in the reserved sriracha sauce, the cilantro, and scallions. Season the rice to taste with salt and transfer to a large serving platter.

Slice the reserved steak into thin slices, somewhere between ¼ to ½ inch (6 to 12 mm) thick. Place the sliced steak on top of the rice, drizzle the fish sauce caramel on top, and sprinkle the dish with bonito flakes (if using) and a bit of extra cilantro. Serve immediately.

Green Jungle Curry Noodles

SERVES 4

FOR THE NOODLE DOUGH:
Dan dan noodle dough (page 112)

FOR THE CURRY:
¼ cup (60 ml) reserved pork fat from the
    Red Roasted Pork Belly (page 218) or
    canola (rapeseed) or vegetable oil
4 scallions (spring onions), ends trimmed,
    thinly sliced, white and green parts
    separated
1 small green bell pepper, halved, seeded,
    and finely chopped
½ small carrot, finely chopped
1 tablespoon minced fresh ginger
2 tablespoons minced fresh lemongrass
    (white part only)
3 large Kaffir lime leaves
6 tablespoons (3 oz/85 g) green curry
    paste
6 cups (1.4 liters) store-bought chicken
    stock (broth)
1 tablespoon sugar
1 large handful cilantro (coriander) leaves
Kosher (coarse) salt

TO SERVE:
All-purpose (plain) flour, for dusting
Kosher (coarse) salt
1 lb (455 g) Red Roasted Pork Belly
    (page 218), thinly sliced
2 heads baby bok choy, leaves separated
    and cores discarded
1 large handful Thai basil leaves, divided
1 handful cilantro (coriander) leaves,
    roughly chopped
1 large handful store-bought crispy fried
    shallots
2 tablespoons ESC Fragrant Chile Oil
    (page 206) or high-quality store-bought,
    for serving

Having successfully made noodles for our *dan dan* noodle dish (see page 112), we wanted to use them in a spicy, brothy green curry dish almost as if the noodles were ramen. When making the noodles, the finer and thinner the noodles, the better (or use store-bought ramen noodles). You could also use sliced chicken breast, shrimp, or large cubes of fish in place of the pork belly—just poach them in the curry until they're cooked through.

MAKE THE NOODLE DOUGH:
Make the noodles as instructed on page 112.

MAKE THE CURRY:
Heat the fat in a large skillet and, when piping hot, add the scallion whites along with the bell pepper, carrot, ginger, lemongrass, Kaffir lime leaves, and curry paste. Cook over medium-high heat, stirring now and then, until the vegetables are softened and the sauce is fragrant, about 10 minutes. Add the stock and sugar and bring the curry to a boil. Reduce the heat and simmer for 20 minutes (use this time to roll out the noodles). Add the cilantro (coriander) and purée the mixture using an immersion blender (or carefully purée it, in batches, in a stand blender and return it to the pot). Season to taste with salt and keep warm over low heat.

TO SERVE:
While the curry is simmering, divide the noodle dough into 4 pieces (so it's easier to roll out). Working with 1 piece at a time (keep the other pieces covered with plastic so that they don't dry out), flour the dough and use a pasta machine (or a rolling pin and a lot of effort) to roll out the noodle dough until it's about as thick as an envelope with a letter in it (ultimately you want your noodles to be chewy, so you don't want the dough rolled too thinly). If you're using a pasta machine, stop at setting 4. Use a linguine cutter to slice the sheets into noodles (or roll up the sheets of pasta like a cigar and slice crosswise with a knife). Toss the noodles with a little bit of flour to keep them from sticking. Repeat the process with the remaining pieces of dough.

Bring a pot of lightly salted water to a boil.

Meanwhile, place a large skillet over high heat. Add the pork and cook, turning the slices, until they're brown and crisp, about 2 minutes on each side.

Add the bok choy and half of the Thai basil to the warm curry.

Add the noodles to the boiling water and boil them until they're tender, about 1 minute. Drain the noodles in a colander and reserve.

Divide the curry among 4 deep bowls, being sure to evenly distribute the bok choy. Divide the noodles between the bowls and top each serving with a quarter of the pork. Sprinkle the rest of the Thai basil, the reserved scallion greens, the cilantro, and crispy shallots over each bowl and drizzle with some of the chile oil. Serve immediately.

Alejandro's Rice Sticks with Steak, Crab, and Spicy Shrimp Paste

SERVES 4

1 tablespoon fish sauce

1 tablespoon sugar

8 oz (230 g) flank steak, thinly sliced
    against the grain

6 oz (170 g) rice sticks (medium-thick,
    labeled *bánh pho viêt mien lão*)

½ tablespoon *gochujang* chile paste

1 tablespoon shrimp (prawn) paste

1 tablespoon *sambal oelek* chile paste

½ teaspoon hoisin sauce

¼ cup (60 ml) canola (rapeseed)
    or vegetable oil

½ small white onion, thinly sliced

1 jalapeño, stemmed and thinly sliced

1 Fresno or other fresh red chile, stemmed
    and thinly sliced

2 heads baby bok choy, leaves separated
    and cores discarded

Kosher (coarse) salt and black pepper

1 cup (100 g) fresh mung bean sprouts

2 large handfuls baby spinach

2 oz (60 g) fresh crabmeat, picked over
    for shells and cartilage

1 large handful cilantro (coriander) leaves,
    roughly chopped

2 scallions (spring onions), ends trimmed,
    thinly sliced

1 small handful each: fresh julienned
    ginger, Thai basil leaves, and store-
    bought crispy fried shallots

½ lime, cut into wedges

Alejandro, our chef at Elizabeth Street Café, has been working with us since before ESC opened its doors. One of the most hilarious people we know, he's the master of throw-everything-together stir-fries and spicy food. This surf-and-turf combination of steak, crab, and spicy shrimp paste is a favorite.

In a medium bowl, whisk together the fish sauce, sugar, and 1 tablespoon water until the sugar is dissolved. Pour the mixture into a large resealable plastic bag and add the steak. Squeeze all the air out of the bag so the marinade completely covers the steak. Refrigerate the meat for at least 1 hour and up to overnight.

Line a plate with a clean cotton dish towel. Put the rice sticks in a large bowl of hot tap water and let them soak until they're softened, about 5 minutes. Drain in a colander (don't rinse them) and transfer to the lined plate.

Whisk together the *gochujang*, shrimp paste, *sambal oelek*, and hoisin in a small bowl and reserve the sauce.

Heat the oil in a large wok, a large seasoned carbon-steel fry pan, or your largest nonstick pan set over high heat until piping hot. (If your pan is small, cook the noodles in 2 batches.) Add the onion and chiles and cook, stirring, until the vegetables are softened and browned in spots, about 3 minutes. Add the marinated flank steak and cook, turning the pieces as they brown, until browned on both sides, 1 to 2 minutes per side. Add the bok choy and cook until it's just wilted, about 2 minutes.

Season the mixture with salt and pepper and add the reserved noodles. Cook, stirring, until the noodles are warmed through and even softer than they were to begin with but still retain a little chew, about 3 minutes. Add the reserved *gochujang* sauce and stir well to combine. Reduce the heat to medium and add the bean sprouts, spinach, crab, cilantro, and scallions. Stir well to combine and cook until the crab is warmed through and the spinach is wilted, about 1 minute. Transfer the noodles to a serving platter. Top with the ginger, Thai basil, and crispy shallots and squeeze the lime half over the noodles. Serve immediately.

Spicy Lamb Dan Dan Noodles with Thai Chile and Mint

SERVES 4

FOR THE NOODLE DOUGH:

2 cups (240 g) all-purpose (plain) flour,
  plus extra for your work surface

2 eggs

1 teaspoon toasted sesame oil

½ teaspoon kosher (coarse) salt

FOR THE LAMB SAUCE:

3 tablespoons ESC Fragrant Chile Oil
  (page 206) or high-quality store-bought

12 oz (340 g) ground lamb

8 scallions (spring onions), ends trimmed,
  thinly sliced and white and green parts
  separated

1 garlic clove, minced

1 tablespoon minced fresh ginger

2 tablespoons finely chopped pickled
  mustard greens

½ cup (120 g) tomato paste (purée)

1 tablespoon sambal oelek chile paste

1 tablespoon gochujang chile paste

2 tablespoons Shaoxing cooking wine
  or dry sherry

2 cups (475 ml) Vietnamese Meat Stock
  (page 216)

Bottom white half of a stalk of fresh
  lemongrass, outer layers peeled off,
  bruised with the back of your knife
  or a mallet

1 sprig Thai basil leaves

Leaves from 1 sprig mint

2 tablespoons fish sauce

1 large handful cilantro (coriander) leaves,
  roughly chopped

TO SERVE:

2 large handfuls Thai basil leaves

2 large handfuls mint leaves

1 large handful cilantro (coriander) leaves,
  roughly chopped

1 cup (100 g) fresh mung bean sprouts

2 tablespoons extra-virgin olive oil

1 lime, cut into wedges

Kosher (coarse) salt and black pepper

1 teaspoon thinly sliced fresh Thai bird
  chile (about 2 chiles)

This is basically an Asian version of spaghetti Bolognese. Substitute fresh chow mein noodles (also called steamed egg or Hong Kong-style noodles) in place of homemade ones. A generous dose of mint at the end is a nod to lamb with mint jelly, a welcome bit of brightness and a counterpoint to the heat. This recipe is contingent on good chile oil as the base of the sauce—we recommend our ESC Fragrant Chile Oil (page 206)— or use a high-quality store-bought one.

MAKE THE NOODLE DOUGH:

Mound the flour on a clean work surface. Make a crater in the center and crack the eggs directly into it along with the sesame oil, salt, and 1 tablespoon water. Use a fork to whisk the egg mixture and slowly push the flour into the egg mixture. Once a thick dough forms, knead the dough by hand. Slowly add 2 more tablespoons water until you have a firm dough ball. Cover the dough with plastic wrap (clingfilm) and refrigerate for at least 40 minutes and up to overnight. If not using within 1 day, place the dough in an airtight bag and freeze for up to 2 weeks (defrost at room temperature before continuing). Reserve the dough.

MAKE THE LAMB SAUCE:

Heat the chile oil in a large skillet over high heat until piping hot, then add the lamb and cook, stirring to break up the meat, until all the pink is cooked out, about 5 minutes. Add the whites of the scallions, the garlic, and the ginger and cook, stirring constantly, until the mixture is fragrant, about 2 minutes. Add the mustard greens and cook just until warmed through, about 1 minute. Add the tomato paste, sambal oelek, and gochujang and cook, stirring, until the mixture is deep red, about 2 minutes. Add the cooking wine and use a wooden spoon to scrape up the bits at the bottom of the pan. Add the stock (broth) and lemongrass and bring the mixture to a boil. Reduce the heat to a simmer and add the Thai basil and mint. Let the mixture simmer, stirring, until thick like a Bolognese sauce, about 25 minutes. Discard the lemongrass, Thai basil, and mint. Stir in the fish sauce and cilantro (coriander) and keep the sauce warm over low heat.

TO SERVE:

Place the Thai basil, mint, cilantro, and bean sprouts in a bowl and drizzle with the olive oil. Squeeze 1 lime wedge over the herbs and toss to combine. Reserve the remaining wedges for serving. Season the salad to taste with salt and pepper and reserve.

Divide the dough into 4 pieces. Working with 1 piece at a time (cover the other pieces with plastic wrap so they don't dry out), flour the dough and use a pasta machine (or a rolling pin) to roll out the dough until it's as thick as an envelope with a letter in it. (You want your noodles to be chewy so don't make the dough too thin.) If using a pasta machine, stop at setting 4. Use a linguine cutter to slice the sheets into noodles (or roll up the sheets of pasta like a cigar and thinly slice crosswise with a knife). Toss the noodles with a bit of flour to keep them from sticking. Repeat with the remaining dough.

Bring a pot of lightly salted water to a boil and cook the noodles in the water until tender, about 1 minute. Drain the noodles in a colander and reserve.

Warm 4 shallow bowls in a 300°F (150°C/Gas Mark 2) oven for 1 minute or in the microwave for 30 seconds. Divide the sauce among the bowls, then place the noodles over the sauce. Divide the herb salad over the noodles and sprinkle with scallion greens and sliced chiles. Serve immediately with the remaining lime wedges on the side.

NOTE: If you don't have Vietnamese Meat Stock (page 216) high-quality store-bought stock and add 1 teaspoon each of kosher (coarse) salt and sugar, 1 whole clove, 1 (1-inch/2.5 cm) cinnamon stick, ¼ star anise, 1 (1-inch/2.5 cm) piece roughly chopped fresh ginger, 1 (3-inch/7.5 cm) square of dried kombu, and 1 tablespoon fish sauce. Simmer the stock for about 25 minutes, then straightthrough a fine-mesh sieve (discard the solids) before proceeding with the rest of the recipe.

Drunken Noodles with Chicken Sausage and Peanuts

SERVES 4

FOR THE CHICKEN SAUSAGE:

2 boneless, skinless chicken thighs
    or ½ lb (230 g) coarsely ground dark
    meat chicken
1 small garlic clove, minced
½ teaspoon minced fresh lemongrass
    (white part only)
½ teaspoon kosher (coarse) salt
¼ teaspoon packed dark brown sugar
¼ teaspoon thinly sliced Thai bird chile
    (about ½ chile)
1 scallion (spring onion), ends trimmed,
    minced
¼ teaspoon fish sauce

FOR THE NOODLES:

8 oz (230 g) dry, very thick rice noodles
    (preferably "XL rice sticks")
⅓ cup (80 ml) hoisin sauce
1 tablespoon sriracha
3 tablespoons fish sauce
1½ tablespoons unseasoned rice vinegar
¼ cup (60 ml) canola (rapeseed) or
    vegetable oil
1 yellow onion, finely diced
1 jalapeño, stemmed and minced
1 Fresno or other fresh red chile, stemmed
    and minced
1 small bunch fresh oyster mushrooms
    (1½ oz/43 g), tough stems discarded,
    roughly chopped
12 fresh shiitake mushrooms (6 oz/170 g),
    stems discarded, roughly chopped
1 large carrot, cut into matchsticks
Kosher (coarse) salt and black pepper
2 large handfuls Thai basil leaves, roughly
    chopped
1 cup (100 g) fresh mung bean sprouts
2 large handfuls cilantro (coriander) leaves,
    roughly chopped, divided
4 scallions (spring onions), ends trimmed,
    thinly sliced, divided
½ cup (60 g) dry roasted peanuts, roughly
    chopped
1 lime, cut into wedges, for serving

These "drunken" noodles are a traditional accompaniment to drinking. The most important are the thick rice noodles and Thai basil. We go through so much Thai basil at the restaurant that we built a small garden behind the restaurant to supply our high demand.

MAKE THE CHICKEN SAUSAGE:

If using whole chicken thighs, trim off and discard any large pieces of fat or tendon. Finely dice the thighs and place the meat in a large bowl with the garlic, lemongrass, salt, brown sugar, Thai chile, scallion, and fish sauce. Mix well with a spoon until the chicken is tacky (you can use a stand mixer fitted with a paddle attachment). Reserve the mixture at room temperature if making the noodles immediately, or cover and refrigerate up to 1 day.

MAKE THE NOODLES:

Put the noodles in a large bowl of hot tap water and let them soak until softened, about 5 minutes. Drain in a colander and transfer the noodles to a clean cotton dish towel (don't use paper towels—the noodles will stick to them). If not using immediately, place a second clean cotton dish towel on top of the noodles and cover with plastic wrap (clingfilm), as it's important to keep the noodles as dry as possible. Refrigerate for up to 2 days.

In a small bowl, whisk together the hoisin, sriracha, fish sauce, and vinegar. Reserve the sauce.

Heat the oil in a large nonstick skillet and, when piping hot, crumble in the chicken mixture and cook over high heat, stirring now and then to break up the meat, until the chicken starts to brown, about 5 minutes. Add the onion, jalapeño, Fresno chile, all the mushrooms, and the carrot, and season with plenty of salt and pepper. Cook, stirring now and then, until the chicken is dark brown and the vegetables are softened, about 5 minutes. Add the reserved noodles and cook until the noodles are translucent and softened but still retain a little bite, about 5 minutes. Add the reserved hoisin mixture and the Thai basil, and stir to combine. Season the noodles to taste with salt and turn off the heat. Add the bean sprouts, half the cilantro, and half the scallions and stir to combine. Transfer the noodles to a serving platter and garnish with the remaining cilantro, scallions, and the peanuts. Serve immediately with lime wedges.

Sticky Rice in Lotus Leaves with Pork, Shiitakes, and Sausage

SERVES 4

¾ lb (340 g) boneless pork shoulder (ask your butcher for a single thinly sliced piece)

3 tablespoons fish sauce, divided

2 tablespoons sugar

1 scallion (spring onion), ends trimmed, thinly sliced

4 large lotus leaves

1 tablespoon sriracha

1 tablespoon unseasoned rice vinegar

2 tablespoons canola (rapeseed) or vegetable oil

12 fresh shiitake mushrooms (6 oz/170 g), stems discarded and caps cut in half

Kosher (coarse) salt

Black pepper

¼ cup (60 ml) extra-virgin olive oil

Cooked sticky rice (page 22 Sticky Rice with Ginger Sausage, Herb Salad, and Poached Egg), cooled to room temperature

¼ cup (60 ml) hoisin sauce

2 links (3 oz/85 g) Chinese cured sausage, thinly sliced

Simple Shaved Cabbage Salad (page 214)

½ cup (120 ml) ESC XO Sauce (page 208)

A traditional dim sum item, this sticky rice, filled with pork and mushrooms and wrapped in fragrant lotus leaves, is often referred to as *lo mai gai*. Great for a dinner party, you can assemble in advance and steam as you greet guests. Simple Shaved Cabbage Salad (page 214) or some quick stir-fried asparagus or green beans, make for a nice side. The lotus leaves infuse the rice with a lot of flavor and aroma, so serve the rice in the leaves and unfold them like placemats.

Place the pork between 2 large pieces of plastic wrap (clingfilm) and, using a mallet or a small heavy pot, gently pound the pork to tenderize and flatten it to about ¼ inch (6 mm) thick.

In a small bowl, combine 2 tablespoons of the fish sauce, the sugar, and the scallion with 2 tablespoons water and whisk together until the sugar dissolves. Combine the sauce and the pork in a large resealable plastic bag. Squeeze all the air out of the bag so that the marinade is completely covering the pork. Refrigerate the meat for at least 4 hours and up to overnight.

In a large bowl of hot tap water, weigh the lotus leaves down with another bowl so that they're fully submerged. Let soak until pliable, about 30 minutes.

Meanwhile, heat a grill or a grill (griddle) pan to high heat. Remove the pork from the marinade and brush off the scallions. Pat the pork dry with paper towels. Reduce the heat to medium-low and grill the pork until charred on both sides and firm to the touch, 2 to 3 minutes per side. Transfer the pork to a plate and let it rest for 10 minutes. Thinly slice the pork and reserve.

Meanwhile, in a small bowl, whisk together the remaining tablespoon of fish sauce, the sriracha, the vinegar, and 2 tablespoons water.

Heat the canola oil in a large skillet and, when piping hot, add the mushrooms, season lightly with salt and pepper, and cook over high heat, stirring now and then, until the mushrooms are browned, about 5 minutes. Add the reserved sriracha sauce and cook, stirring, until the mushrooms are nicely glazed, about 3 minutes. Transfer the mushrooms to a plate and let them cool.

Drain the lotus leaves, unfold them if they're folded in half (they usually are) and spread them out over a clean work surface, green side facing up. Drizzle 1 tablespoon of the olive oil on each lotus leaf and use your hands to coat the surface with the oil. Divide the rice among the lotus leaves and drizzle 1 tablespoon of hoisin over each portion of rice. Top the rice with some of the pork, mushrooms, and Chinese sausage. Fold each *lo mai gai* up tightly as if you were creating an envelope around a letter. The rice and the fillings should be completely encased with the lotus leaf. You can secure each one with a piece of twine if you'd like, or just make sure they're seam side down when you steam them so that they stay closed.

Get the steamer going again and transfer the *lo mai gai* to it, seam sides down. Steam until fragrant and the fillings are heated through (you can test by piercing one of the *lo mai gai* with the blade of a paring knife and touching it to test the temperature), about 8 minutes. Transfer the *lo mai gai*, seam side up, to serving plates.

Open up each *lo mai gai* and put a small pile of the cabbage salad next to each one. Serve each plate with a small ramekin of XO sauce and remind your guests not to eat the lotus leaves. Serve immediately.

Vietnamese Yellow Curry with Mussels and Chicken Meatballs

SERVES 4

FOR THE CURRY STOCK (BROTH):

4 tablespoons (60 g) butter

6 tablespoons yellow curry paste

½ yellow bell pepper, halved, seeded, and finely diced

½ medium carrot, finely diced

3 scallions (spring onions), ends trimmed, thinly sliced

½ jalapeño, stemmed and minced

2 tablespoons minced fresh ginger

2 tablespoons minced fresh lemongrass (white part only)

½ small white onion, finely diced

2 Kaffir lime leaves

6 cups (1.4 liters) Vietnamese Meat Stock (page 216) made with chicken bones or high-quality store-bought chicken stock (broth)

1 tablespoon fish sauce

1 tablespoon sugar

FOR THE MEATBALLS:

1 lb (455 g) ground dark meat chicken

1½ teaspoons kosher (coarse) salt

½ teaspoon fish sauce

¼ teaspoon sugar

1 large garlic clove, minced

1 scallion (spring onion), white part only, minced

1 teaspoon minced fresh lemongrass (white part only)

1 fresh Thai bird chile, minced

1 large handful cilantro (coriander) leaves, finely chopped

TO SERVE:

2 lb (1 kg) fresh mussels, debearded

½ small head cauliflower (9 oz/250 g), cut into florets

2 small or 1 large kohlrabi, peeled and cut into thin strips

2 large handfuls cilantro (coriander) leaves, divided

2 Fresno or other fresh red chiles, stemmed and thinly sliced

Toasted Classic French Baguette (page 164) or high-quality store-bought, or Stovetop Jasmine Rice (page 212), for serving

To honor the French cafe side of ESC's personality, we have mussels on the menu as a nod to *moules-frites*. We developed this rich yellow curry with plenty of mussels and delicious little chicken meatballs for added heft. Like our Escargots with Thai Basil–Curry Butter (page 98), this curry is a wonderful excuse to eat a lot of crusty French bread.

MAKE THE CURRY STOCK (BROTH):

In a large pot set over medium heat, melt the butter, then add the curry paste, bell pepper, carrot, scallions, jalapeño, ginger, lemongrass, onion, and Kaffir lime leaves. Cook, stirring now and then, until the vegetables are softened but not browned, about 10 minutes. Add the stock, bring to a boil, then reduce the heat and simmer until the stock is reduced slightly and the curry is fragrant, 20 minutes (use this time to prepare the meatballs). Purée the mixture using an immersion blender (or carefully purée it, in batches, in a stand blender and return it to the pot) and stir in the fish sauce and sugar. Turn off the heat and reserve the curry stock.

MAKE THE MEATBALLS:

Line a sheet pan with plastic wrap (clingfilm) or parchment paper. Set a large bowl over a larger bowl filled with ice (this will help keep the mixture cold as you prepare it) and, using wet hands (to keep the mixture from sticking), combine the chicken, salt, fish sauce, sugar, garlic, scallion, lemongrass, chile, and cilantro. Using a teaspoon to help you portion the meatballs, form the mixture into 32 small (½ oz/15 g) meatballs. Transfer the meatballs to the lined sheet pan and place in the freezer for 15 minutes (this will help the meatballs retain their round shape).

TO SERVE:

Bring the yellow curry back up to a boil and add the semifrozen meatballs. Cook, stirring a couple of times, until the meatballs are firm to the touch, about 12 minutes. Add the mussels, cauliflower, and kohlrabi and cover the pot. Cook until the mussels open, about 5 minutes. Pick out and discard any mussels that haven't opened. Add half the cilantro to the curry and stir to combine. Transfer the curry to 4 large bowls, being sure to evenly distribute the meatballs, mussels, and vegetables. Sprinkle each bowl with scilantro and sliced chiles. Serve immediately with baguette or rice.

Crispy Pork and Shrimp Crêpe with Bean Sprouts

SERVES 4

FOR THE CRÊPE BATTER:

1½ cups (165 g) nonglutinous white rice flour

1 tablespoon cornstarch (cornflour)

½ teaspoon kosher (coarse) salt

½ teaspoon sugar

½ teaspoon ground turmeric

¼ teaspoon Madras curry powder

1 (13.5 oz/398 ml) can full-fat coconut milk, well shaken

FOR THE FILLING:

12 oz (340 g) pork belly, cut into ½-inch (1 cm) dice

½ white onion, thinly sliced

12 oz (340 g) shrimp (prawns), shelled and deveined, cut into ½-inch (1 cm) dice

¼ cup (60 ml) sriracha

2 tablespoons fish sauce

1 tablespoon granulated sugar

TO SERVE:

Canola (rapeseed) or vegetable oil, as needed

2 cups (200 g) mung bean sprouts

4 scallions (spring onions), ends trimmed, thinly sliced

1 head iceberg lettuce, quartered

1 head red leaf lettuce

1 large handful mint leaves and stems

1 large handful Thai basil leaves and stems

1 large handful cilantro (coriander) leaves and stems

Hoisin sauce, for serving

Sriracha, for serving

1 cup (240 ml) Nuoc Cham (page 208), for serving

A lot of people will judge a Vietnamese restaurant by its crispy, savory crêpe, much like judging a Texas barbecue spot by its brisket or ribs. We prepare our crêpes traditionally. Eating Vietnamese crêpes is all about different temperatures and textures. With so many flavors in a single bite, these crêpes are fun and delightfully messy.

MAKE THE CRÊPE BATTER:

Put the rice flour, cornstarch, salt, sugar, turmeric, and curry powder in a large bowl and whisk to combine. Whisk in the coconut milk and ¾ cup (180 ml) cold water until the batter is smooth. Let the mixture sit at room temperature for 1 hour before using or cover and refrigerate for up to 3 days. (The batter will settle and separate so be sure to whisk it and also bring it to room temperature before proceeding.)

MAKE THE FILLING:

In a large heavy skillet set over high heat, add the pork belly and cook, stirring, until the pork is crisp and the fat is rendered, about 5 minutes. Using a slotted spoon, transfer the pork to a small bowl and reserve. Pour off all but 2 tablespoons of the fat (reserve the excess for another use) and add the sliced onion to the skillet. Reduce the heat to medium and cook the onion slices, stirring, until they're translucent, about 5 minutes. Return the reserved pork belly to the pan along with the shrimp, sriracha, fish sauce, and sugar and cook, stirring, until the shrimp are firm to the touch, about 2 minutes. Reduce the heat to low to keep the filling warm while you prepare the crêpes.

TO SERVE:

Set a large black steel crêpe pan or heavy-bottomed nonstick pan over medium-high heat and add enough oil to lightly coat the surface. Give the batter a good stir and carefully pour a quarter of it (about ¾ cup/180 ml) evenly over the surface of the pan. Swirl the pan so that the batter coats it evenly. Cook until small holes form on the top and the bottom begins to brown, about 1 minute. Drizzle 1 tablespoon oil over the surface of the crêpe, reduce the heat to low, and cook until the underside of the crêpe is browned (check by lifting with a spatula) and the top is totally opaque and fully cooked, about 5 minutes.

Put a quarter of the shrimp mixture on one side of the crêpe and top with ½ cup (50 g) of the bean sprouts and a quarter of the sliced scallions. Fold the unfilled side of the crêpe over the filling and transfer it to a plate. Repeat the process 3 more times.

Put a quarter wedge of iceberg lettuce, a few leaves of red leaf lettuce, and some of each of the herbs next to each plated crêpe. Serve immediately with hoisin and sriracha and a small bowl of *nuoc cham* alongside.

Whole Steamed Fish with Black Vinegar, Ginger, and Lime

SERVES 4

FOR THE BLACK VINEGAR SAUCE:

¼ cup (60 ml) black vinegar

2 tablespoons soy sauce

2 tablespoons *sambal oelek* chile paste

1 tablespoon honey

2 tablespoons thinly sliced fresh ginger

1 teaspoon fresh lime juice

FOR THE FISH:

2 scallions (spring onions), ends trimmed, thinly sliced on a long bias

1 tablespoon canola (rapeseed) or vegetable oil

One (2 lb/1 kg) whole flounder, scaled and gutted

1 teaspoon kosher (coarse) salt

½ teaspoon black pepper

1 lime, thinly sliced

1 Thai bird chile, thinly sliced

Spicy Kohlrabi and Ginger Salad (page 213), for serving

Stovetop Jasmine Rice (page 212), for serving

Whole fish in Vietnamese restaurants and home kitchens prepared are all sorts of ways: roasted, deep-fried, grilled (griddled), and more. Our favorite method is to gently steam the fish, which is easy to prepare. We use flounder in the recipe below, but a whole branzino, snapper, or any other non-oily fish would work well. If you don't have a steamer large enough, you could bake the fish on a sheet pan in a 350°F (175°C/Gas Mark 4) oven. The black vinegar in the sauce, available in any Asian grocery store and online, lends a distinctive flavor and is worth seeking out.

MAKE THE BLACK VINEGAR SAUCE:

Combine the vinegar, soy sauce, *sambal oelek*, honey, and ginger in a small pot set over medium heat. Simmer and stir the sauce until the honey is dissolved and the ginger is tender, about 5 minutes. Remove from the heat, stir in the lime juice, and reserve the mixture.

MAKE THE FISH:

Place the scallions in a small bowl of ice water and let them soak while you prepare the fish.

Set up a conventional steamer or a bamboo steamer inside of a large pot and fill the pot with water accordingly. Line the steamer with a piece of parchment paper and drizzle with the oil. Rub the oil to coat the surface of the parchment. Bring the water up to a boil.

Make a deep cut down the center of the spine of the fish, which runs from the center of the tail to the center of the head, and season both sides of the fish with the salt and pepper. Transfer the fish to the prepared steamer, cover, and steam until the fish is firm to the touch and the flesh is opaque and flakes easily when pierced with a paring knife, about 15 minutes.

Pour the reserved vinegar sauce on a large serving platter and tilt to cover the surface of the platter. Spread the ginger from the sauce evenly over the surface of the platter. Using 2 silicone spatulas to help you, lift the fish from the steamer and carefully transfer it on top of the ginger and the sauce. Drain the scallions and scatter them over the fish along with the sliced lime and chile. Serve the fish immediately with the salad and rice on the side.

DESSERT

Blueberry Croissant Bread Pudding with Blueberry Sauce

SERVES 8

FOR THE BLUEBERRY SAUCE:

3 cups fresh (400 g) or frozen (340 g)
   blueberries, raspberries, or blackberries
1 tablespoon fresh lemon juice
¾ cup (150 g) sugar
Pinch of kosher (coarse) salt

FOR THE BREAD PUDDING:

1 lb (455 g) croissants, torn into bite-size
   pieces (about 11 cups)
10 egg yolks
3 cups (720 ml) heavy (whipping) cream
1 cup (240 ml) milk
¾ cup (150 g) sugar
½ teaspoon kosher (coarse) salt
2 teaspoons vanilla extract
1 cup fresh (130 g) or frozen (115 g)
   blueberries, divided

This is a traditional bread pudding, but since it's made with croissants, it's extra delicious. Like so many of our dishes, this was created out of a need to use up leftovers. At the restaurant, we serve the pudding with a scoop of cilantro (coriander) ice cream. To make the ice cream at home, blend a large handful of cilantro leaves into the base of our Double Vanilla Ice Cream (page 144) before churning it.

MAKE THE BLUEBERRY SAUCE:
Place the blueberries and lemon juice in a medium pot set over medium heat. When the blueberries begin to burst, add the sugar and salt and reduce the heat to medium-low. Let the sauce cook, stirring now and then, until all the blueberries release their juice and the sauce is syrupy, about 20 minutes. Turn off the heat and reserve the sauce. To serve the sauce warm, gently reheat it over low heat before serving.

MAKE THE BREAD PUDDING:
Preheat the oven to 325°F (160°C/Gas Mark 3).
   Place the croissant pieces on a sheet pan and bake, stirring a couple times, until the pieces dry out and turn and light brown, about 10 minutes. Let cool to room temperature.
   Whisk the egg yolks in a bowl and set aside.
   Place the heavy cream, milk, sugar, and salt in a saucepan set over medium heat. Heat the mixture until bubbles form around the edge and, while whisking constantly, cook just until the sugar is dissolved, about 5 minutes. Ladle about 1 cup (240 ml) of the hot milk mixture into the egg yolks and whisk to combine. Then ladle another 1 cup (240 ml) of the milk mixture into the egg yolks and whisk again to combine. Pour the remainder of the milk mixture into the egg yolks and give the mixture a final whisk to combine. You are tempering the yolks, gradually warming without cooking them, which ensures that the custard remains smooth.
   Strain the custard through a fine-mesh sieve into a clean medium bowl. Stir in the vanilla extract and let the custard cool to room temperature.
   Place the cooled croissant pieces into a 9 × 13-inch (23 × 33 cm) ovenproof dish. Pour half of the custard over the croissant pieces and add half of the blueberries; refrigerate the remaining custard. Use your hands to gently combine. Refrigerate the croissant mixture until the croissant pieces have absorbed the custard, about 30 minutes.
   Bring a kettle of water to a boil.
   Pour the remaining custard mixture over the soaked croissants and sprinkle the top of the bread pudding with the remaining blueberries. Place the dish with the pudding in a larger ovenproof dish, then add the hot water to the base of the larger dish so it comes halfway up the sides. Carefully transfer the the pudding in the waterbath to the oven and bake until set (test for doneness by pressing down on the bread pudding with a spoon to check that no custard comes up from the sides), 60 to 70 minutes.
   Serve the bread pudding and the blueberry sauce warm or at room temperature.

Vietnamese Coffee Pots de Crème

MAKES 6

2½ cups (600 ml) heavy (whipping) cream, divided

½ cup (120 ml) milk

Pinch of kosher (coarse) salt

2 tablespoons ground chicory coffee

6 egg yolks

1 (7 oz/198 g) can sweetened condensed milk

6 Chocolate Five-Spice Macarons (page 154), for serving

Cocoa powder, for dusting

Vietnamese coffee, with its contrasting mix of bitter chicory flavor and sweet condensed milk, in and of itself could be considered dessert. To turn it into a lush custard, we combined the two star ingredients with cream and eggs. Our favorite brand of chicory coffee is Café du Monde from New Orleans.

Preheat the oven to 325°F (160°C/Gas Mark 3).

Bring a kettle of water to a boil, then remove from the heat and reserve.

In a saucepan set over medium heat, combine 1½ cups (360 ml) heavy cream, milk, and salt and warm until bubbles form around the edge. Stir in the coffee grounds, turn off the heat, and let steep for 15 minutes.

Place the egg yolks in a medium bowl and whisk to combine. While continuing to whisk, slowly pour the warm cream mixture into the egg yolks. Whisk in the condensed milk. Line a fine-mesh sieve with a double layer of cheesecloth and pour the custard through it into a large pitcher (jug). Note that a coffee filter or nut milk bag can be used in place of the cheesecloth.

Evenly distribute the custard among 6 (6 to 8 oz/177 to 240 ml) ramekins. Wrap each ramekin tightly with plastic wrap (clingfilm) and then aluminum foil (this will keep them airtight and prevent a skin from forming during baking). Set the ramekins in a large roasting pan, leaving a little space between each one. Pour the hot water in the base of the pan so it comes halfway up the sides of the ramekins.

Transfer the *pots de crème* to the oven and bake until set, 45 minutes. To test, unwrap a ramekin and lightly shake it—the mixture should jiggle when done. If still loose, continue to bake for another 5 minutes and check again. Carefully remove the roasting pan from the oven and let the *pots de crème* cool in the water bath until they reach room temperature. Transfer the *pots de crème* to the refrigerator and let chill for at least 6 hours and up to overnight before serving.

When ready to serve, in a cold bowl, whip the remaining 1 cup (240 ml) heavy cream until stiff peaks form. Garnish the *pots de crème* cold with a macaron each, add a dollop of whipped cream, and dust with cocoa powder before serving.

Pineapple Tarte Tatin

SERVES 8

2 tablespoons (30 g) butter

6 tablespoons sugar, divided

1 large ripe pineapple, peeled, cored, and cut into rounds ½ inch (1 cm) thick

1 sheet puff pastry, defrosted

Tarte tatin, the apple pie of France, was originally named after a French country inn called the Hôtel Tatin. It is customarily made with apples cooked in a skillet with caramel, topped with puff pastry, and then, once baked, inverted. We wanted to put a Southeast Asian spin on this French classic and swapped apples for pineapple and the result is like the easiest pineapple upside-down cake, since you don't have to make a cake batter. Look for high-quality, all-butter, store-bought puff pastry in your grocery store. To gild the lily, we serve this tart with whipped cream and lots of Star Anise Caramel Sauce (page 134), but the tart is just as great on its own or with Palm Sugar Ice Cream (page 149), Double Vanilla Ice Cream (page 144), or crème fraîche.

Preheat the oven to 375°F (190°C/Gas Mark 5). Line a sheet pan with parchment paper and set aside.

Melt the butter in an 8-inch (20 cm) stainless-steel skillet set over medium heat. Sprinkle 2 tablespoons of the sugar over the butter and carefully place half of the pineapple rings into the pan (you can break a pineapple slice into pieces to fill the gaps) and let them cook until the undersides are browned, about 5 minutes. Carefully transfer the rings to a plate, being sure to leave the juice in the pan. Sprinkle another 2 tablespoons of the sugar over the surface of the pan and place the remaining pineapple rings in the pan. Cook this second batch until its undersides are browned, about 3 minutes. Turn off the heat. Return the first pineapple batch to the pan, browned sides down, arranging all the rings in a snug concentric circle. (Overlapping is okay and it's good to have a few layers of pineapple because the fruit will cook down in the oven.)

Cut the piece of puff pastry into a 10-inch (25 cm) circle; discard the trimmings or bake them alongside the tarte tatin as a snack. Place the puff pastry round over the pineapple and tuck the edges into the skillet. Evenly sprinkle the final 2 tablespoons of sugar over the top of the puff pastry and transfer the skillet to the lined sheet pan (this will catch any drips).

Bake the tart until the pastry is dark golden brown, the sugar is caramelized, and the pineapple juices below bubbling, about 50 minutes.

Transfer the skillet to a wire rack and let the tart rest until the skillet handle is cool to the touch. Carefully invert the tart onto a serving platter (delicious juice will come out of the pan, so use a platter much larger than the skillet and with a rim to catch the juice). Cut the tart into wedges and serve immediately.

Star Anise Caramel Sauce

MAKES 1 CUP (240 ML)

¾ cup (150 g) sugar
Pinch of cream of tartar
2 whole star anise
¾ cup (180 ml) heavy (whipping) cream
½ teaspoon kosher (coarse) salt

Easily the most delicious topping for Pineapple Tarte Tatin (page 132), this sauce is also the perfect thing to make a bowl of vanilla ice cream really special.

In a small pot set over medium-high heat, combine the sugar, cream of tartar, star anise, and 2 tablespoons water. Cook the caramel, swirling but not stirring the pot now and then, until the caramel turns the color of a copper penny, about 10 minutes. Very carefully add the heavy cream and salt. The cream will bubble vigorously when it hits the hot caramel, so stand back.

Reduce the heat to low and stir until the sauce is smooth (some caramel might seize when the cool cream hits, but it will dissolve with a little stirring and gentle heat). Once the sauce is smooth, turn off the heat and let the sauce cool in the pot, so the star anise flavor has time to develop.

To serve, gently warm the sauce over low heat, remove and discard the star anise, and drizzle over whatever you like (or just eat with a spoon). Store the cooled sauce in an airtight container in the refrigerator for up to 1 week. Warm the sauce over low heat before serving.

Pâte à Choux Puffs for Profiteroles, Cream Puffs, and Eclairs

MAKES BATTER FOR
24 PROFITEROLES, 12 CREAM PUFFS,
OR 18 ÉCLAIRS

8 tablespoons (115 g) butter
1 tablespoon sugar
1 teaspoon kosher (coarse) salt
1 cup (120 g) all-purpose (plain) flour
4 eggs

Learning to make *pâte à choux*, a classic French pastry dough, opens up all sorts of pastry possibilities. Instead of folding together butter and flour, *choux* is made by stirring water, butter, and flour together over heat and then beating eggs into it. The resulting thick batter can be piped into any shape and bakes into crisp, airy puffs that can be filled with all sorts of different pastry creams or ice cream and drizzled with chocolate and strawberry sauces (page 136). You can add cheese to the batter and make *gougères*. For all the *pâte à choux* recipes that follow, you can work ahead and freeze the puffs after piping and before baking. Freeze them on the sheet pan, then transfer to an airtight bag. Store the puffs in the freezer for up to one month, then bake them frozen and add a few extra minutes in the oven.

Preheat the oven to 375°F (190°C/Gas Mark 5). Line a sheet pan with parchment paper and set aside.

In a medium pot set over high heat, combine the butter, sugar, and salt with 1 cup (240 ml) water and bring to a boil. Remove the pot from the heat and, using a wooden spoon, thoroughly stir in the flour. Return the pot to the stove and set it over medium heat. Cook the mixture, stirring constantly, until it pulls away from the sides of the pot and a film forms on bottom of pan, about 1 minute.

Transfer the mixture to the bowl of a standing electric mixer fitted with the paddle attachment. Mix on medium-low speed until slightly cooled, about 2 minutes. Raise the speed to medium, add the eggs 1 at a time, and mix until a soft peak forms when you touch the batter, about 1 more minute once all the eggs have been added. The batter should be smooth and shiny.

Transfer the batter to a resealable plastic bag and snip off one of the corners so that the opening is at least ¼ inch (6 mm) wide (or use a pastry [piping] bag fitted with a #10 tip).

For profiteroles, pipe the batter onto the prepared sheet pan to form 24 even rounds (each should be about 1½ inches/4 cm in diameter), evenly spaced apart.

For cream puffs, pipe the batter onto the prepared sheet pan to form 12 even rounds (each should be about 3 inches/7.5 cm in diameter), evenly spaced apart.

For éclairs, pipe the batter onto the prepared sheet pan to form 18 oblong rectangles (each should be about 4½ inches/12 cm long and 1 inch/2.5 cm thick), evenly spaced apart.

Bake the *pâte à choux* until golden brown, firm to the touch, and puffed up, 30 to 35 minutes. Transfer the puffs to a wire rack to cool before filling.

Profiteroles with Strawberry-Yuzu and Chocolate Sauces

SERVES 8

FOR THE STRAWBERRY-YUZU SAUCE:

½ cup (100 g) granulated sugar

2 tablespoons yuzu juice

2 cups (260 g) strawberries, hulled and roughly chopped

FOR THE CHOCOLATE SAUCE:

½ cup (60 g) unsweetened cocoa powder

½ cup (100 g) granulated sugar

¼ teaspoon kosher (coarse) salt

1½ cups (360 ml) heavy (whipping) cream

3 tablespoons (45 g) cold butter, diced

½ teaspoon vanilla extract

TO SERVE:

24 baked and cooled profiterole-size Pâte à Choux Puffs (page 135)

8 scoops Double Vanilla Ice Cream (page 144) or store-bought

8 scoops Spicy Ginger Ice Cream (page 146) or store-bought

8 scoops Fresh Strawberry Ice Cream (page 149) or store-bought

Powdered (icing) sugar, for dusting

We find that three profiteroles per person—one filled with Double Vanilla Ice Cream (page 144), another with Spicy Ginger Ice Cream (page 146), and the last with Fresh Strawberry Ice Cream (page 149)—make a perfect portion. You can vary the ice cream flavors and use any type of store-bought ice cream. To put these profiteroles over the edge, we serve them over plenty of fresh strawberry sauce and top with the warm chocolate sauce.

MAKE THE STRAWBERRY-YUZU SAUCE:

In a small pot set over high heat, combine the granulated sugar with ¼ cup plus 2 tablespoons (90 ml) water and bring to a boil; stir to dissolve the sugar. Transfer the syrup to a bowl and let it cool to room temperature. Stir in the yuzu and strawberries and let the sauce sit and marinate while you prepare the chocolate sauce.

MAKE THE CHOCOLATE SAUCE:

Off heat, place the cocoa powder, granulated sugar, and salt in a small pot along with ½ cup (120 ml) of the heavy cream. Whisk together to form a thick paste and then, while whisking, slowly pour in the rest of the heavy cream. Add the butter and set the pot over low heat. Cook the sauce, stirring constantly, until the butter is incorporated and the sauce is warm, about 2 minutes. Stir in the vanilla and keep the sauce warm over the low heat.

TO SERVE:

Divide the strawberry sauce evenly among 8 individual serving plates. Cut or break each puff in half and put a scoop of ice cream on the bottom half of each puff. Top each scoop of ice cream with the top halves of the puffs and transfer them to the plates (be sure to put one of each flavor on each dish). Drizzle the warm chocolate sauce over the profiteroles, dust with powdered (icing) sugar and serve immediately.

Store the remain cooled sauces in airtight containers in the refrigerator for up to 3 days. Serve the strawberry-yuzu sauce at room temperature or warmed over low heat. Warm the chocolate sauce over low heat, whisking to combine in case it separates.

Vanilla Pastry Cream, Our Way

MAKES 3 CUPS (690 G)

¼ cup (36 g) cornstarch (cornflour)

2 eggs

1½ teaspoons vanilla bean paste

¼ teaspoon kosher (coarse) salt

¾ cup (150 g) sugar

1 cup (240 ml) milk

1½ cups (360 ml) heavy (whipping) cream, divided

This pastry cream is our go-to "plain" filling for cream puffs (pages 139 and140) and éclairs (pages 139 and 143) and it's the base recipe for our flavored fillings. Our method of making pastry cream is a little different—we like to fold unsweetened whipped cream into the pastry cream, lightens the texture and tempers its sweetness. This also helps the final cream puffs and éclairs from becoming too thick and pasty. Pastry cream freezes well, so you can double the recipe and store extra.

Place a large glass or stainless steel bowl in the freezer.

In a large bowl, whisk together the cornstarch, eggs, and vanilla bean paste and reserve.

In a saucepan set over medium heat, combine the salt, sugar, milk, and 1 cup (240 ml) of the heavy cream and warm, whisking constantly, until the sugar dissolves and bubbles form around the edge, about 2 minutes. Ladle a little of the hot milk mixture into the egg mixture and whisk to combine; then ladle another little bit of the hot milk mixture into the egg mixture and whisk again to combine. Pour the warmed egg mixture into the remaining milk mixture in the saucepan and bring to a simmer, stirring constantly with a wooden spoon to make sure the pastry cream doesn't scorch on the bottom, until the custard mixture is thick enough to coat the back of the spoon, about 4 minutes. Immediately remove the saucepan from the heat and continue to stir vigorously until the pastry cream gets thicker, about 1 minute.

Remove the bowl from the freezer. Press the pastry cream through a fine-mesh sieve into the chilled bowl and stir to help it cool down. Set the bowl over a bowl of ice water (make sure the water doesn't come into contact with the pastry cream). Cover the pastry cream with plastic wrap (clingfilm), pressing the plastic directly onto the surface of the mixture to prevent a skin from forming. Let it sit until the pastry cream is at room temperature.

Meanwhile, place the remaining ½ cup (120 ml) heavy cream in a large bowl and whisk by hand or with an electric mixer until stiff peaks form.

Add one-third of the whipped cream into the room temperature pastry cream and stir to combine. Add another third of the whipped cream and carefully fold the cream into the pastry cream, being careful not to deflate the mixture. Fold in the final third of whipped cream. Use the pastry cream immediately or store in an airtight container in the refrigerator for up to 1 day (or freeze for up to 1 month).

Toasted Coconut Cream Puffs

MAKES 12

1 recipe Vanilla Pastry Cream, Our Way
(opposite page)

¾ cup (60 g) sweetened shredded coconut,
toasted

12 baked and cooled cream puff-size Pâte
à Choux Puffs (page 135)

A cream puff is a light, crispy *pâte à choux* puff filled with airy pastry cream. You
can make these with just Vanilla Pastry Cream, Our Way (opposite page), but folding
in some toasted coconut makes them even more special.

In a large bowl, combine the pastry cream and the coconut and fold together.

Cut or break each puff in half and divide the coconut pastry cream among
the bottom halves of each puff. Place the top halves of the puffs on top and serve
immediately or refrigerate for up to 6 hours before serving.

Pistachio Éclairs with Matcha Ganache

MAKES 18

1 cup (130 g) shelled pistachios, lightly
toasted

¼ cup (50 g) sugar

2 tablespoons canola (rapeseed) oil

½ teaspoon kosher (coarse) salt

1 recipe Vanilla Pastry Cream, Our Way
(opposite page)

18 baked and cooled éclair-size Pâte à
Choux Puffs (page 135)

6 oz (170 g) white chocolate chips

2 tablespoons (30 g) butter, at room
temperature

½ teaspoon matcha powder

These éclairs taste like pistachio ice cream served from a scoop that was just in
the green tea ice cream container. The hint of matcha in the white chocolate ganache
topping perfectly complements the nutty pistachio filling, plus you get two shades
of green in one delicious éclair. If you can find pistachio paste (sold at some baking
supply stores), feel free to substitute it for the ground nut mixture.

Place the pistachios, sugar, oil, and salt in the bowl of food processor and pulse until
finely chopped, then let the machine run until the mixture turns into a thick paste that
clumps together, about 1 minute.

Transfer the pistachio paste to a large bowl, add one-third of the pastry cream,
and stir together. Add the remaining pastry cream and fold together gently.

Cut or break each puff in half and divide the pistachio pastry cream among the
bottom halves of each puff. Top with the remaining halves and set aside.

Place the white chocolate and butter in a microwave-safe bowl and microwave
in 30-second increments, stirring in between, until the chocolate is totally melted.
Stir in the matcha powder. Evenly spread the ganache on top of the filled éclairs,
and set aside for about 10 minutes, until the ganache hardens. Serve immediately
or refrigerate for up to 6 hours before serving.

Espresso Cream Puffs

MAKES 12

¼ cup (36 g) cornstarch (cornflour)

2 eggs

1½ teaspoons vanilla bean paste

1½ cups (360 ml) heavy (whipping) cream, divided

1 cup (240 ml) milk

¾ cup (150 g) sugar

3 tablespoons finely ground espresso

¼ teaspoon kosher (coarse) salt

12 baked and cooled cream puff–size Pâte à Choux Puffs (page 135)

Since strong coffee is a pastry's best friend, we figured we'd put the two together to make the ultimate treat. The filling packs a caffeinated punch (great in the morning), so if you're serving these for dessert after dinner, feel free to use decaffeinated coffee.

Place a large glass or stainless steel bowl in the freezer.

In a large bowl, whisk together the cornstarch, eggs, and vanilla bean paste and reserve.

In a saucepan set over medium heat, combine 1 cup (240 ml) of the heavy cream, the milk, sugar, espresso, and salt, and warm the mixture, whisking constantly, until the sugar dissolves and bubbles form around the edge, about 2 minutes.

Line a fine-mesh sieve with a double layer of cheesecloth and pour the mixture through it into a large pitcher (jug). Note that a coffee filter or nut milk bag can be used in place of the cheesecloth. Discard the contents of the sieve and rinse out the pot.

Slowly pour the hot milk mixture into the egg mixture, whisking constantly. Return the custard to the cleaned-out pot and set it over medium-low heat. Simmer, stirring constantly with a wooden spoon to make sure the pastry cream doesn't scorch on the bottom, until the custard mixture is thick enough to coat the back of the spoon, about 4 minutes.

Remove the bowl from the freezer. Press the pastry cream through a fine-mesh sieve into the chilled bowl and stir to help it cool down. Cover the pastry cream with plastic wrap (clingfilm), pressing the plastic right onto the surface of the mixture to prevent a skin from forming, and let it sit until it reaches room temperature.

Meanwhile, place the remaining ½ cup (120 ml) of heavy cream in a large bowl and whisk by hand or with an electric mixer until stiff peaks form.

Add one-third of the whipped cream into the room-temperature pastry cream and stir to combine. Add another third of the whipped cream and carefully fold the cream into the lightened pastry cream, being careful not to deflate the mixture. Fold in the final third of whipped cream.

Cut or break each puff in half and divide the espresso pastry cream among the bottom halves of each puff. Place the top halves of the puffs on top and serve immediately or refrigerate for up to 6 hours before serving.

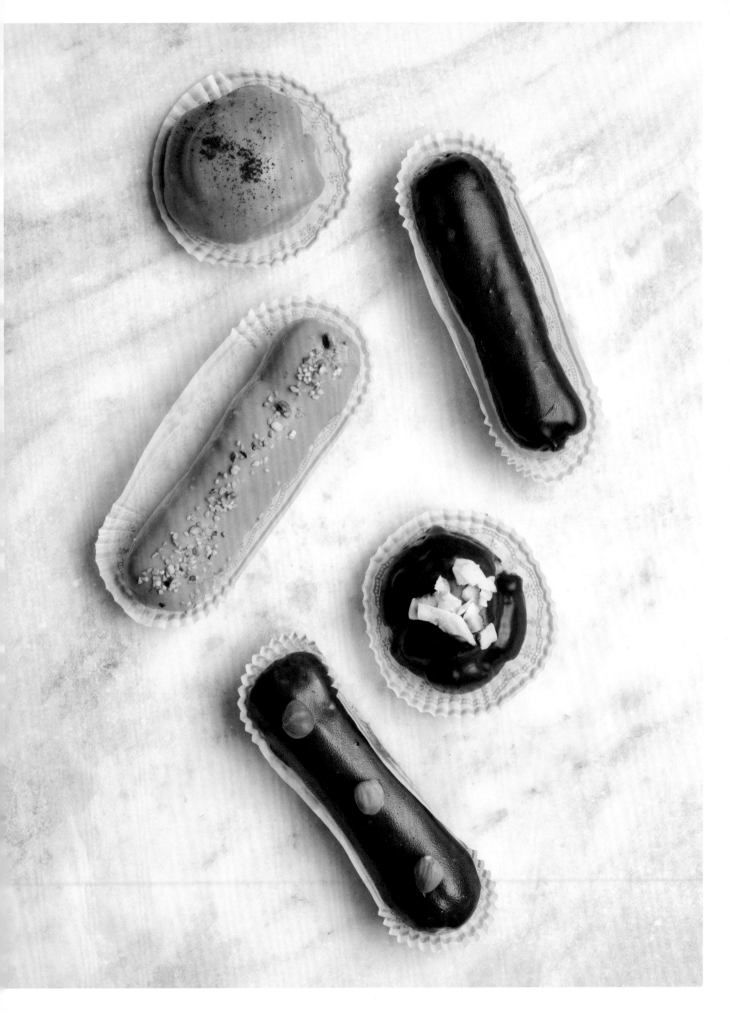

Nutella Éclairs with Milk Chocolate Ganache

MAKES 18

¼ cup (50 g) sugar

2 egg whites

½ cup (150 g) hazelnut cocoa spread
(preferably Nutella)

½ cup (120 g) crème fraîche

18 baked and cooled éclair-size Pâte à
Choux Puffs (page 135)

4 oz (115 g) milk or dark chocolate chips

¼ cup (60 ml) heavy (whipping) cream

This is our only pâte à choux treat that doesn't use pastry cream as a base for its filling. Instead, Swiss meringue is folded with Nutella and crème fraîche to create a light mousse filling. For the ganache, you could substitute dark chocolate for the milk chocolate. For extra texture, you can top each éclair with candied hazelnuts from the crêpes on page 46.

Bring a small pot of water to a boil, then reduce to a simmer. Place the sugar and egg whites in a glass or stainless-steel bowl and set it on top of the pot (make sure the water doesn't touch the bowl). Stir the mixture until the sugar is completely dissolved (test by rubbing some of the mixture between your fingers), about 1 minute. Transfer the mixture to the bowl of a standing electric mixer fit with a whisk attachment. Whisk on high speed until the meringue is bright white, stiff, and glossy, about 2 minutes.

In a large bowl, whisk together the hazelnut cocoa spread and crème fraîche. Add one-third of the meringue to the mixture and whisk to combine. Carefully, as not to deflate it, fold in another third of the meringue, then the final third. Cover the bowl and refrigerate for at least 1 hour and up to overnight, before filling the éclairs.

Cut or break each puff in half lengthwise and divide the meringue filling among the bottom halves of each puff. Top with the remaining puffs and set aside.

Place the chocolate chips in a large bowl. Pour the heavy cream in a small saucepan over medium heat and warm until the bubbles form around edges, about 3 minutes. Pour the hot cream over the chocolate and let the cream warm the chocolate, about 30 seconds. Stir together until all the chocolate is melted and the ganache is smooth. Drizzle the ganache over the éclairs and set aside for 10 minutes, letting the chocolate harden. Serve immediately or refrigerate for up to 6 hours before serving.

Double Vanilla Ice Cream

MAKES ABOUT 1 QUART (1 LITER)

8 egg yolks
2 cups (475 ml) milk
2 cups (475 ml) heavy (whipping) cream
1 cup (200 g) sugar
¼ cup (60 ml) light corn syrup
½ teaspoon kosher (coarse) salt
1 tablespoon plus 1 teaspoon vanilla bean
   paste
1 teaspoon vanilla extract

We like our ice cream so lush and rich that you can almost chew it, and we make it in-house. Ice creams and sorbets are easy to make at home and the results are better than just about anything you can buy. Good technique is key: carefully and patiently temper egg yolks, and then cook the custard until thick—and your ice cream will taste creamy and luxurious.

In a medium bowl, whisk the egg yolks and reserve.

In a large saucepan set over medium heat, combine the milk, heavy cream, sugar, corn syrup, and salt and, whisking constantly, warm the mixture until bubbles form around the edges and the sugar is dissolved, about 2 minutes. Ladle about 1 cup (240 ml) of the hot milk mixture into the egg yolks and whisk to combine and then ladle another 1 cup (240 ml) of the milk mixture into the egg yolks and whisk again to combine. Pour the warmed egg yolk mixture into the remaining milk mixture in the saucepan and simmer, stirring constantly with a wooden spoon, until the custard mixture is thick enough to coat the back of the spoon, about 4 minutes.

Strain the custard through a fine-mesh sieve into a bowl set over a larger bowl of ice water. Whisk in the vanilla bean paste and the vanilla extract. Let the custard cool to room temperature, then cover and refrigerate until cold, at least 4 hours and up to overnight.

Stir the custard and transfer it to an ice cream machine. Churn according to the manufacturer's instructions. Serve immediately while the ice cream has the texture of soft serve or transfer to an airtight container and freeze until hardened, about 4 hours. Store in the freezer for up to 2 weeks. Let the ice cream soften at room temperature for about 10 minutes before serving.

Banana and Five-Spice Powder Ice Cream

MAKES ABOUT 1 QUART (1 LITER)

4 egg yolks
1 cup (240 ml) milk
1 cup plus 2 tablespoons (270 ml) heavy (whipping) cream
¾ cup (150 g) sugar
3 tablespoons light corn syrup
2½ teaspoons five-spice powder
½ teaspoon kosher (coarse) salt
4 medium or 3 large very ripe bananas
1½ teaspoons fresh lemon juice
1½ teaspoons vanilla extract

In a medium bowl, whisk the egg yolks and reserve.

In a large saucepan set over medium heat, combine the milk, heavy cream, sugar, corn syrup, five-spice powder, and salt and, whisking constantly, warm the mixture until bubbles form around the edges and the sugar is dissolved, about 2 minutes. Ladle about 1 cup (240 ml) of the hot milk mixture into the egg yolks and whisk to combine and then ladle another 1 cup (240 ml) of the milk mixture into the egg yolks and whisk again to combine. Pour the warmed egg yolk mixture into the remaining milk mixture in the saucepan and simmer, stirring constantly with a wooden spoon, until the custard is thick enough to coat the back of the spoon, about 4 minutes.

Strain the custard through a fine-mesh sieve into a bowl set over a larger bowl of ice water. Let the mixture cool to room temperature.

Meanwhile, place the bananas in a food processor and purée until smooth. Whisk the bananas into the cooled custard and add the lemon juice and vanilla. Cover the custard and refrigerate until cold, at least 4 hours and up to overnight.

Stir the custard and transfer it to an ice cream machine. Churn according to the manufacturer's instructions. Serve immediately while the ice cream is the texture of soft serve or transfer to an airtight container and freeze until hardened, about 4 hours. Store in the freezer for up to 2 weeks. Let the ice cream soften at room temperature for about 10 minutes before serving.

Mango-Lime Sorbet

MAKES ABOUT 1 QUART (1 LITER)

1 cup (200 g) sugar
½ teaspoon kosher (coarse) salt
1½ pounds (680 g) mangoes, peeled, pitted, and roughly chopped (about 3 small or 2 large mangoes)
¼ cup plus 2 tablespoons (90 ml) fresh lime juice

In a small saucepan set over high heat, combine the sugar and salt with 1¼ cups (300 ml) water and cook, stirring, just until the sugar and salt are dissolved, about 2 minutes. Turn off the heat and let the mixture cool to room temperature.

Transfer the syrup to a blender or food processor and add the mangoes and lime juice. Purée until smooth. Transfer the purée to a large container, cover, and refrigerate for at least 2 hours and up to overnight.

Transfer the purée to an ice cream machine and churn according to the manufacturer's instructions. Serve immediately or transfer to an airtight container and freeze until hardened, about 4 hours. Store in the freezer for up to 2 weeks. Let the sorbet soften at room temperature for about 10 minutes before serving.

Spicy Ginger Ice Cream

MAKES ABOUT 1 QUART (1 LITER)

8 egg yolks
2 cups (475 ml) milk
2 cups (475 ml) heavy (whipping) cream
1 cup (200 g) sugar
¼ cup (60 ml) light corn syrup
½ teaspoon kosher (coarse) salt
½ packed cup (70 g) finely chopped fresh
   ginger

In a medium bowl, whisk together the egg yolks and reserve.

In a large saucepan set over medium heat, combine the milk, heavy cream, sugar, corn syrup, salt, and ginger and, whisking constantly, warm the mixture until bubbles form around the edges and the sugar is dissolved, about 2 minutes. Ladle about 1 cup (240 ml) of the hot milk mixture into the egg yolks and whisk to combine and then ladle another 1 cup (240 ml) of the milk mixture into the egg yolks and whisk again to combine. Pour the warmed egg yolk mixture into the remaining milk mixture in the saucepan and simmer, stirring constantly with a wooden spoon, until the custard mixture is thick enough to coat the back of the spoon, about 4 minutes.

Strain the custard through a fine-mesh sieve into a bowl set over a larger bowl of ice water. Let the custard cool to room temperature, then cover and refrigerate until cold, at least 4 hours and up to overnight.

Strain the custard through a fine-mesh sieve, pressing down on the ginger to extract as much flavor as possible, and transfer to an ice cream machine. Churn according to the manufacturer's instructions. Serve immediately while the ice cream is the texture of soft serve or transfer to an airtight container and freeze until hardened, about 4 hours. Store in the freezer for up to 2 weeks. Let the ice cream soften at room temperature for about 10 minutes before serving.

White Miso Ice Cream

MAKES ABOUT 1 QUART (1 LITER)

8 egg yolks
2 cups (475 ml) milk
2 cups (475 ml) heavy (whipping) cream
¾ cup (150 g) sugar
¼ cup (70 g) white miso paste

In a medium bowl, whisk the egg yolks and reserve.

In a large saucepan set over medium heat, combine the milk, heavy cream, sugar, and miso paste and, whisking constantly, warm until the mixture forms bubbles around the edges and the sugar is dissolved, about 2 minutes. Ladle about 1 cup (240 ml) of the hot milk mixture into the egg yolks and whisk to combine and then ladle another 1 cup (240 ml) of the milk mixture into the egg yolks and whisk again to combine. Pour the warmed egg yolk mixture into the remaining milk mixture in the saucepan and simmer, stirring constantly with a wooden spoon, until the custard is thick enough to coat the back of the spoon, about 4 minutes.

Strain the custard through a fine-mesh sieve into a bowl set over a larger bowl of ice water. Let the custard cool to room temperature, then cover and refrigerate until cold, at least 4 hours and up to overnight.

Stir the custard and transfer it to an ice cream machine. Churn according to the manufacturer's instructions. Serve immediately while the ice cream is the texture of soft serve or transfer to an airtight container and freeze until hardened, about 4 hours. Store in the freezer for up to 2 weeks. Let the ice cream soften at room temperature for about 10 minutes before serving.

Saigon Cinnamon Ice Cream

MAKES ABOUT 1 QUART (1 LITER)

8 egg yolks
2 cups (475 ml) milk
2 cups (475 ml) heavy (whipping) cream
1 cup (200 g) sugar
½ teaspoon kosher (coarse) salt
2 teaspoons ground Saigon cinnamon

In a medium bowl, whisk the egg yolks and reserve.

In a large saucepan set over medium heat, combine the milk, heavy cream, sugar, salt, and cinnamon and, whisking constantly, warm the mixture until bubbles form around the edges and the sugar is dissolved, about 2 minutes. Ladle about 1 cup (240 ml) of the hot milk mixture into the egg yolks and whisk to combine and then ladle another 1 cup (240 ml) of the milk mixture into the egg yolks and whisk again to combine. Pour the warmed egg yolk mixture into the remaining milk mixture in the saucepan and simmer, stirring constantly with a wooden spoon, until the custard is thick enough to coat the back of the spoon, about 4 minutes.

Strain the custard through a fine-mesh sieve into a bowl set over a larger bowl of ice water. Let the mixture cool to room temperature, then cover and refrigerate until cold, at least 4 hours and up to overnight.

Stir the custard and transfer to an ice cream machine. Churn according to the manufacturer's instructions. Serve immediately while the ice cream is the texture of soft serve or transfer to an airtight container and freeze until hardened, about 4 hours. Store in the freezer for up to 2 weeks. Let the ice cream soften at room temperature for about 10 minutes before serving.

Coconut-Lemongrass Sorbet

MAKES ABOUT 1 QUART (1 LITER)

½ cup (100 g) sugar
½ teaspoon kosher (coarse) salt
1 stalk lemongrass (white part only), outer layers peeled off, halved and bruised with the back of your knife or a mallet
¾ cup (180 ml) well-shaken full-fat coconut milk
2 cups (475 ml) coconut purée
2 tablespoons light corn syrup
1 tablespoon fresh lime juice
1 tablespoon lemon-flavored vodka (preferably Absolut Citron)

In a small saucepan set over high heat, combine the sugar, salt, and lemongrass with ½ cup (120 ml) water and cook, stirring, just until the sugar and salt are dissolved, about 2 minutes. Turn off the heat and let the mixture steep for at least 1 and up to 4 hours to allow the lemongrass to infuse the syrup.

Strain the syrup through a fine-mesh sieve into a large bowl (discard the lemongrass) and whisk in the coconut milk, coconut purée, corn syrup, lime juice, and vodka. Cover and refrigerate until cold, at least 2 hours and up to overnight.

Stir the mixture and transfer to an ice cream machine. Churn according to the manufacturer's instructions. Serve immediately or transfer to an airtight container and freeze until hardened, about 4 hours. Store in the freezer for up 2 weeks. Let the sorbet soften at room temperature for about 10 minutes before serving.

NOTE: If you can't track down coconut purée, increase the coconut milk to 2 cups (475 ml) and purée it with 1 cup (80 g) unsweetened shredded coconut flakes and ½ teaspoon high-quality coconut extract.

Palm Sugar Ice Cream

MAKES ABOUT 1 QUART (1 LITER)

8 egg yolks
2¼ cups (540 ml) milk
2¼ cups (540 ml) heavy (whipping) cream
11½ oz (325 g) palm sugar
½ teaspoon kosher (coarse) salt

In a medium bowl, whisk the egg yolks and reserve.

In a large saucepan set over medium heat, combine the milk, heavy cream, palm sugar, and salt and, whisking constantly, warm until bubbles form around the edges and the sugar is dissolved, about 5 minutes. Ladle about 1 cup (240 ml) of the hot milk mixture into the egg yolks and whisk to combine and then ladle another 1 cup (240 ml) of the milk mixture into the egg yolks and whisk again to combine. Pour the warmed egg yolk mixture into the remaining milk mixture in the saucepan and simmer, stirring constantly with a wooden spoon, until the custard is thick enough to coat the back of the spoon, about 4 minutes.

Strain the custard through a fine-mesh sieve into a bowl set over a larger bowl of ice water. Let the mixture cool to room temperature, then cover and refrigerate until cold, at least 4 hours and up to overnight.

Stir the custard and transfer to an ice cream machine. Churn according to the manufacturer's instructions. Serve immediately while the ice cream is the texture of soft serve or transfer to an airtight container and freeze until hardened, about 4 hours. Store in the freezer for up to 2 weeks. Let the ice cream soften at room temperature for about 10 minutes before serving.

Fresh Strawberry Ice Cream

MAKES ABOUT 1 QUART (1 LITER)

6 egg yolks
¾ cup (180 ml) milk
1 cup plus 2 tablespoons (270 ml) heavy (whipping) cream
¾ cup (150 g) sugar
3 tablespoons light corn syrup
½ teaspoon kosher (coarse) salt
3 cups (400 g) strawberries, hulled
2 teaspoons yuzu juice or fresh lemon juice

In a medium bowl, whisk the egg yolks and reserve.

In a large saucepan set over medium heat, combine the milk, heavy cream, sugar, corn syrup, and salt and, whisking constantly, warm the mixture until bubbles form around the edges and the sugar is dissolved, about 2 minutes. Ladle about 1 cup (240 ml) of the hot milk mixture into the egg yolks and whisk to combine and then ladle another 1 cup (240 ml) of the milk mixture into the egg yolks and whisk again to combine. Pour the warmed egg yolk mixture into the remaining milk mixture in the saucepan and simmer, stirring constantly with a wooden spoon, until the custard is thick enough to coat the back of the spoon, about 4 minutes.

Strain the custard through a fine-mesh sieve into a bowl set over a larger bowl of ice water. Let the custard cool to room temperature.

Meanwhile, place the strawberries in a food processor and purée until smooth. Whisk the strawberries into the cooled custard along with the yuzu juice. Cover the custard and refrigerate until cold, at least 4 hours and up to overnight.

Stir the custard and transfer it to an ice cream machine. Churn according to the manufacturer's instructions. Serve immediately while the ice cream is the texture of soft serve or transfer to an airtight container and freeze until hardened, about 4 hours. Store in the freezer for up to 2 weeks. Let the ice cream soften at room temperature for about 10 minutes before serving.

Vietnamese Coconut Sundae

SERVES 4

FOR THE COCONUT AND AGAVE SYRUP:

1 cup (240 ml) well-shaken full-fat
   coconut milk

¼ cup plus 2 tablespoons (90 ml) agave
   syrup

½ teaspoon kosher (coarse) salt

2 Kaffir lime leaves, roughly chopped

2 tablespoons chopped fresh ginger

½ stalk lemongrass (white part only),
   outer layers peeled off, bruised with
   the back of your knife or a mallet
   and roughly chopped

FOR THE STICKY RICE:

1 cup (220 g) Thai sticky rice or any sweet,
   glutinous rice, rinsed well

2 Kaffir lime leaves, bruised with the back
   of your knife or a mallet

TO SERVE:

2 young coconuts, husked

Crushed ice

4 generous scoops Coconut-Lemongrass
   Sorbet (page 148)

1 large handful assorted flavors of coconut
   jellies (page 224), finely diced if they
   aren't already

1 ripe mango, peeled, pitted, and diced

1 large handful Thai basil leaves

1 Thai bird chile, thinly sliced

1 lime

In Vietnam, sweetened sticky rice is often served for dessert. We intensified the flavor with the addition of coconut milk, Kaffir lime, lemongrass, and ginger. Served with a scoop of Coconut-Lemongrass Sorbet (page 148) and a variety of fun toppings—mango, coconut jelly candies (sweets) (page 224), Thai basil, and a little unexpected chile—this is easily our most fun, and dare we say it, one of the best vegan desserts ever made.

MAKE THE COCONUT AND AGAVE SYRUP:

In a small saucepan set over high heat, combine the coconut milk, agave syrup, salt, Kaffir lime leaves, ginger, and lemongrass and bring to a boil. Immediately reduce the heat and simmer, stirring now and then, until the syrup has reduced slightly, about 8 minutes. Remove from the heat and let the syrup cool to room temperature in the saucepan. Strain the syrup through a fine-mesh sieve into a small bowl and set aside (discard the aromatics).

MAKE THE STICKY RICE:

Set up a conventional or a bamboo steamer inside of a large pot and fill the pot with water accordingly. Bring the water up to a boil over high heat. Put the rice and the Kaffir lime leaves into a shallow pan or dish that fits comfortably inside of the steamer. Make sure the pan or dish is large enough so that the rice only comes about ¼ inch (6 mm) up the dish. Pour enough cool water into the dish just to cover the rice by ½ inch (1 cm). Put the dish of rice and water into the steamer, cover the steamer, and cook until the rice is tender, 20 to 25 minutes. Transfer the rice to a larger bowl and discard the Kaffir lime leaves. Add the syrup mixture and mix well to combine. Let the rice cool to room temperature.

TO SERVE:

Working with 1 coconut at a time, carefully hit it in the center with the back of a knife, rotating the coconut between each hit, until the coconut breaks in half. Fill 4 shallow bowls with crushed ice and rest a coconut half, cracked side up, in each bowl. Divide the sticky rice and the coconut-lemongrass sorbet among the coconut shells. Evenly distribute the coconut jellies, diced mango, Thai basil leaves, and sliced chile among the sundaes. Using a fine grater (like a Microplane), grate the zest from the lime directly over the sundaes. Serve immediately.

Vanilla Macarons with Vanilla Bean Buttercream

MAKES 24

FOR THE SHELLS:

1¼ cups (130 g) almond flour (sometimes labeled "almond meal")

1¾ cups (225 g) powdered (icing) sugar

3 extra-large egg whites, at room temperature

¼ cup plus 1 tablespoon (60 g) granulated sugar

¼ teaspoon vanilla extract

¼ teaspoon cream of tartar

¼ teaspoon kosher (coarse) salt

¼ teaspoon meringue powder (optional, but highly recommended for stability)

FOR THE VANILLA BEAN BUTTERCREAM FILLING:

1 extra-large egg white, at room temperature

¼ cup (50 g) granulated sugar

Pinch of kosher (coarse) salt

½ teaspoon vanilla bean paste or the beans from ½ vanilla bean pod

4 tablespoons (60 g) butter, cut into pieces, at room temperature

Hands down our most popular sweet, not only are *macarons* the perfect two-bite treat after a big bowl of noodles, but their bright colors and seemingly infinite flavor combinations reflect the spirited variety we try to offer at Elizabeth Street Café. They are also gluten-free. See pages 154 and 155 for different versions, all which are based on our master recipe, this basic vanilla *macaron*. While these adorable cookies are incredibly temperamental and can elude and enrage even the most experienced bakers (we speak from experience), the following recipe has been tested for great results at home. The egg whites in this recipe should preferably come from extra-large eggs. After you pipe the *macarons*, you can decorate their shells with sprinkles or colored sugar before baking. *Macarons* are best served cold, as the buttercream will be firm and easier to eat.

MAKE THE SHELLS:

Preheat the oven to 275°F (140°C/Gas Mark 1). Line 2 large sheet pans with parchment paper and set aside. In a large bowl, whisk together the almond flour and powdered sugar and reserve.

Add the egg whites to the bowl of a stand electric mixer fitted with a whisk attachment and whisk on medium-high speed until frothy. Add the granulated sugar, vanilla extract, cream of tartar, salt, and meringue powder (if using). Increase the speed to the high and whisk until the mixture is white, glossy, and forms stiff peaks, stopping occasionally to scrape down the sides of the bowl, about 2 minutes.

Turn off the machine and, using a silicone spatula, stir one-third of the reserved almond flour mixture into the whipped egg whites. Gently fold another third of the almond flour mixture to the egg whites until incorporated. Gently fold in the remaining almond flour mixture until incorporated.

Transfer the meringue to a large resealable plastic bag and snip off one of the corners so that the opening is at least ½ inch (12 mm) wide (or use a pastry [piping] bag fitted with a #12 tip). Pipe 1-inch (2.5 cm) rounds of the meringue evenly spaced apart onto the prepared sheet pans. The meringues should be about ¼ inch (6 mm) thick. Pick up each sheet pan with one hand and tap the bottom with the other to knock out any air bubbles (but don't pick it up and drop it on the counter because the meringues will deflate too much). Wet your fingertips and gently smooth out any little peaks on top of the shells.

Put the sheet pans in the oven and immediately turn up the oven to 300°F (150°C/Gas Mark 2). Bake, rotating the pans from top to bottom and vice versa halfway through baking, until the shells are dry, about 20 minutes. Remove the sheet pans from the oven and let the shells cool completely on wire racks.

MAKE VANILLA BEAN BUTTERCREAM FILLING:

While the meringues are baking, in a large stainless-steel bowl set over a pot of simmering water on the bottom, combine the egg white, sugar, salt, and vanilla (make sure the water doesn't touch the bottom of the bowl). Hold the bowl with a kitchen towel with one hand and whisk vigorously with the other until the sugar is dissolved (test by rubbing some of the mixture between your fingers). Remove the bowl from the double boiler (dry the bottom of the bowl with a kitchen towel so no condensation ends up in your filling). Transfer the mixture to the bowl of a stand mixer fitted with a whisk attachment. Set the mixer to high speed and whisk until the egg whites are bright white, fluffy, and glossy—and doubled in size, 2 to 3 minutes. Reduce the mixer speed to low and incorporate the butter a little at a time until the buttercream filling is completely smooth and shiny.

Cover the bowl with plastic wrap (clingfilm) and transfer the filling to the refrigerator to cool for 1 hour (it will firm as it cools). You can make the filling ahead and refrigerate it, covered, for up to 2 days. Let the filling sit at room temperature for 1 hour before filling the *macarons*.

ASSEMBLE THE MACARONS:

Transfer the filling to a large resealable plastic bag and snip off one of the corners so that the opening is at least ½ inch (12 mm) wide (or use a pastry [piping] bag fitted with a #12 tip). Turn 1 tray of the shells upside down so their flat sides face up. Pipe about 1 tablespoon of the filling on the flat sides of the shells, then sandwich them with the shells from the other tray. Refrigerate the *macarons* for at least 4 hours before serving (they're best cold). Store in a covered, but not completely airtight, box or container for up to 2 days.

Macaron Variations

STRAWBERRY MACARONS:

Add 1 tablespoon strawberry milk powder to the shell mixture along with the almond flour.

Top the shells with pink sprinkles before baking.

Fill with strawberry buttercream: make the Vanilla Bean Buttercream (page 152) but without the vanilla bean paste and add ¼ cup (35 g) finely chopped strawberries while mixing the buttercream to fully incorporate the strawberries and to yield a light pink buttercream without any chunks of berries.

FOR CHAMOMILE AND STRAWBERRY MACARONS:

Add 1 teaspoon ground dried chamomile flowers to the shell mixture along with the almond flour and, after the meringue is at its stiff peak stage, add 3 drops gold gel food coloring.

Top the shells with gold sprinkles before baking.

Fill with strawberry buttercream (from Strawberry Macarons, above).

CHOCOLATE AND FIVE-SPICE MACARONS:

Add 1 tablespoon unsweetened cocoa powder and 1½ teaspoons five-spice powder to the shell mixture along with the almond flour.

Top the shells sparingly with cacao nibs before baking.

Fill with dark chocolate ganache: Finely chop 4 oz (85 g) dark chocolate, place in a bowl, and pour over ¼ cup (60 ml) hot heavy (whipping) cream. Stir to melt the chocolate, then transfer the ganache to a large resealable plastic bag and snip off one corner so the opening is at least ½ inch (12 mm) wide (or use a pastry [piping] bag fit with a #12 tip). Let the ganache cool in the bag until it is firm.

BLACK SESAME MACARONS:

Add 2 teaspoons ground black sesame seeds to the shell mixture along with the almond flour and, after the meringue is at its stiff peak stage, add 2 drops toasted sesame oil.

Top the shells with black sesame seeds before baking.

Fill with sesame buttercream: Make the Vanilla Bean Buttercream (page 152), but without the vanilla bean paste and add 1½ teaspoons toasted sesame oil and ½ teaspoon toasted black sesame seeds toward the end of mixing the buttercream.

LAVENDER MACARONS:

Add a pinch of ground lavender flower to the shell mixture along with the almond flour and, after the meringue is at its stiff peak stage, add 1 drop violet gel food coloring and 1 drop soft pink gel food coloring.

Top the shells with white sprinkles before baking.

Fill with Vanilla Bean Buttercream (page 152).

SAIGON CINNAMON AND MADRAS CURRY MACARONS:

Add 1 teaspoon ground Saigon cinnamon to the shell mixture along with the almond flour.

Fill with Madras curry buttercream: Make the Vanilla Bean Buttercream (page 152), but without the vanilla bean paste, and add 1½ teaspoons Madras curry powder toward the end of mixing the buttercream.

GREEN TEA MACARONS:

Add a pinch of ground green tea leaves or matcha powder to the shell mixture along with the almond flour and, after the meringue is at its stiff peak stage, add 1 drop avocado gel food coloring.

Fill with matcha buttercream: Make the Vanilla Bean Buttercream (page 152), but without the vanilla bean paste, and add 1 teaspoon matcha powder toward the end of mixing the buttercream.

TOASTED COCONUT MACARONS:

Substitute half of the almond flour with coconut flour.

Top the shellssparingly with unsweetened coconut chips before baking.

Fill with Vanilla Bean Buttercream (page 152).

BLUEBERRY AND VIOLET MACARONS:

Add 1 teaspoon blueberry powder to the shell mixture along with the almond flour and, after the meringue is at its stiff peak stage, add 1 drop violet gel food coloring.

Top the shells with silver coarse sugar before baking.

Fill with blueberry buttercream: Make the Vanilla Bean Buttercream (page 152) but without the vanilla bean paste, and add 2 drops violet extract and 2 tablespoons of blueberry jam toward the end of mixing the buttercream.

GRAPEFRUIT AND FENNEL MACARONS:

Add ½ teaspoon dried fennel pollen and the finely grated zest of 1 grapefruit to the shell mixture along with the almond flour and, after the meringue is at its stiff peak stage, add 1 drop soft pink gel food coloring and 1 drop orange food coloring.

Top the shells with pastel green sprinkles before baking.

Fill with grapefruit fennel buttercream: Make the Vanilla Bean Buttercream (page 152), but without the vanilla bean paste, and add the finely grated zest of ½ grapefruit, ½ teaspoon of dried fennel pollen, and 1 table-spoon of grapefruit syrup* toward the end of mixing the buttercream.

THAI BASIL AND PASSION FRUIT MACARONS:

Add a small handful of minced Thai basil leaves to the shell mixture along with the almond flour.

Fill with passion fruit buttercream: Make the Vanilla Bean Buttercream (page 152), but without the vanilla bean paste, and add 1½ tablespoons of passion fruit syrup* toward the end of mixing the buttercream

*To make ½ cup (120 ml) passion fruit syrup, combine ½ cup (120 ml) passion fruit purée and ¼ cup plus 2 tablespoons (75 g) sugar in a small saucepan and bring it to a boil. Then reduce to a simmer and cook on low until the liquid is reduced to ½ cup (120 ml).

Big Mac Ice Cream Sandwich

MAKES 12

Vanilla Macarons with Vanilla Bean
    Buttercream (page 152)
Ice cream of your choice (pages 144-149)

Since summer lasts for about six months in Austin, we're always looking for decadent-but-refreshing desserts. Ice cream sandwiches made from oversize *macaron* shells and filled with our homemade ice creams (because the only thing that's more delicious than buttercream is ice cream) are a no-brainer.

Use a bag with an opening at least ½ inch (12 mm) wide (or use a pastry (piping) bag fitted with a #12 tip) to pipe any variation of macaron shells into 2-inch (5 cm) rounds that are about ½ inch (12 mm) thick and double the recommended baking time. Once they've cooled down, sandwich 2 shells with any type of ice cream. Soften the ice cream at room temperature before filling (at the restaurant, we put softened ice cream in a piping bag). Freeze the filled sandwiches so that they hold together. Before serving, let the sandwiches sit at room temperature for a few minutes, to let them soften a bit.

MACARON LIST

If Elizabeth Street Café had a mascot it would either be George of the Jungle or a variety of *macaron* since both are colorful and a little unexpected. Jen Tucker and Alex Manley, our original bakers and the "mac queens," came up with thousands of flavor combinations. Here are just a few they could remember.

strawberry sprinkle
matcha and strawberry
strawberries and cream
Thai basil and strawberry
black pepper and roasted strawberry
carrot cake
ginger carrot
blueberry cilantro (coriander)
blueberry coconut
blueberry pancakes
Thai basil and blueberry
Thai basil and dark chocolate
Mexican chocolate
Szechuan chocolate
Vietnamese coffee
Chinese five spice
rocky road
macadamia nut and white chocolate
cashew caramel
wasabi lime
lemon meringue pie
cheesecake
chai pecan pie
five-spice pecan praline
pistachio matcha
brown butter kabocha
pecan and kabocha
five-spice kabocha
pumpkin pie
chai brown butter
chai vanilla bean
chai peach
grapefruit and honey
chocolate and passion fruit
key lime pie
pistachio honey
pistachio beet (beetroot)
lime, sea salt, and prickly pear
lime and coconut
salted caramel and brown butter
olive oil and sea salt
banana pudding
beet (beetroot), orange, fennel
orange creamsicle
salted plum
sesame matcha
sesame brown butter

miso and sesame
espresso vanilla
chocolate
caramel
matcha and honey
matcha and peach
miso and peach
miso and plum
miso and brown butter
miso and white chocolate
miso and dark chocolate
miso and honey
miso and banana
miso and macadamia
raspberry chipotle
matcha and plum
ginger plum
ginger peach
lemon poppy
matcha and lemon
chocolate and curry
chamomile, honey, and black pepper
raspberry lychee rose
lavender blueberry
Szechuan raspberry
lavender vanilla
French toast
cinnamon curry (maybe best flavor ever)
Thai chili and honey
Thai chili and raspberry
Thai chili and prickly pear
Thai chili and lemongrass
lemongrass and coconut
ginger lemongrass
Kaffir lime and coconut
red velvet
birthday cake
s'more
caramel, peanut, and chocolate
Thai basil and peanut
peanut butter and jelly
jelly donut
salty dog
dark and stormy
painkiller
piña colada
eggnog

BAKERY

Classic French Baguette

MAKES 4 LOAVES

1½ cups (180 g) bread (strong white) flour

1 teaspoon active dry yeast

8 cups (960 g) high-protein bread (strong white) flour, plus extra for your work surface

2½ tablespoons kosher (coarse) salt

Cooking spray

Calling something a classic French baguette is a tall order, and our original bakers spent a lot of time perfecting this recipe, which boasts that beautifully crisp and crackly crust by which baguettes are measured. Making your own is doable, fun, and gives you a great sense of accomplishment.

In the bowl of a stand mixer, combine the bread flour and yeast with ¾ cup (180 ml) water and, using a wooden spoon, stir the dough together until no lumps remain. Cover the bowl loosely with plastic wrap (clingfilm) or a kitchen towel and let it sit overnight somewhere not too warm and free from drafts (so not near a door or window). This mixture is called "poolish".

Pour 2 cups (475 ml) water on the poolish, then gently place the high-protein flour on top of the water. Lock the bowl into the base of a stand mixer fitted with a dough hook. Mix on low speed until a shaggy dough ball forms, about 1 minute. If the dough is crumbly and very dry, add more water, 1 tablespoon at a time, until it just comes together. If the dough seems too wet, add more flour, 1 tablespoon at a time, until it just comes together. Turn off the mixer and cover the bowl with a kitchen towel. Let the dough rest at room temperature for 30 minutes.

Uncover the dough, add the salt, and mix on medium speed until the dough is smooth, shiny, and passes the windowpane test (see Note at the end of the recipe), about 7 minutes. If your mixer has any trouble mixing the dough evenly, knead vigorously by hand for about 10 minutes. Whether you use a machine or knead by hand, if the dough resists and is difficult to work with, let it rest for a few minutes before proceeding.

Dust your work surface with flour and transfer the dough to it. Pat the dough into a rough rectangle with your hands. Fold each corner of the dough into the center and then turn the dough over so the seams are on the bottom. Cover the dough with a kitchen towel and let it rest for 15 minutes. Repeat the process 3 more times with 15 minutes of rest between each round of folding. Spray a large bowl with cooking spray and transfer the folded dough to the bowl. Cover the dough bowl with plastic wrap and refrigerate for at least 12 and up to 24 hours.

Let the dough rest at room temperature for 1 hour. Lightly flour your work surface and turn the dough out onto it. Using a knife or a bench scraper, evenly divide the dough into 4 (15 oz/425 g) pieces. Form each portion into a *boule* (a smooth ball) by shaping each piece of dough into a rectangle and then gathering the corners of the dough into the center to form a little bundle. Turn each bundle upside down so the seams are on the bottom and the smooth surface is on top. Cup the ball of dough with your hands and roll the dough in tight circles on your work surface to create a tight seam on the bottom and a tense, smooth surface on top. Once you've formed all 4 *boules*, cover them again with the kitchen towel and let them rest for 30 minutes.

Uncover the dough and turn each *boule* upside down so that the seams are facing you. Flatten each piece of dough slightly with your hands so that it roughly resembles a rectangle. With a short side facing you, fold the top of the dough toward its center and press down and then pick up this now larger end and fold it down toward the bottom of the rectangle. You should now have a thick log with one single seam at the bottom.

Give the log a few rolls to form a tight cylinder measuring 12 inches (30 cm) long. Apply a little extra pressure at the ends so they're slightly tapered. Transfer the loaves to a sheet pan or preferably, a baguette pan (a perforated metal pan with indentations that helps baguettes brown and take shape), seam side down. Cover the loaves with a kitchen towel and put the pan in the warmest spot in your kitchen until the rolls are puffed up and doubled in size, about 3 hours.

Preheat the oven to 450°F (230°C/Gas Mark 8) and put a baking dish on the bottom rack of the oven.

Uncover the bread. Using a bread lame (or very sharp paring knife or serrated knife), make 5 even slashes among each loaf, each about ¼ inch (.5 cm) deep.

Place 6 ice cubes in the baking dish in the oven (these will evaporate and create steam when you bake the bread, which will prevent the crust on each loaf from getting too hard) and transfer the bread to the oven on their baguette pan. Bake the baguettes, rotating the pan halfway through so that the loaves brown evenly, until golden brown, 16 to 18 minutes.

Transfer the loaves to a wire rack to cool completely before eating (easier said than done). Leftovers can be stored in an airtight bag at room temperature and toasted before serving or warmed in a 300°F (150°C/Gas Mark 2) oven.

NOTE: The windowpane test—tear off a small piece of dough, stretch it in your hands, and if it stretches to a thinness where you see light through it without tearing, it passes. If it tears before that point, continue to knead the dough.

Bánh Mì Rolls

MAKES 10 ROLLS

6¾ cups (810 g) high-protein bread (strong white) flour, plus extra for your work surface

1½ tablespoons kosher (coarse) salt

1 tablespoon sugar

1½ teaspoons active dry yeast

3 tablespoons vital wheat gluten

3 tablespoons vegetable shortening

When we started making *bánh mì*, we knew we needed the best-quality Vietnamese-style baguette rolls, soft on the inside and crisp on the outside. We minimally mix the dough, which helps keep the crust tender without overworking the gluten. Traditionally, Vietnamese-style bread often uses milk and butter to keep the dough soft. Though these rolls are made with mostly the same ingredients and techniques as our Classic French Baguette (page 164), thanks to the small amount of vital wheat gluten added to the dough, the texture is preserved and the bread is vegan.

In a bowl of a stand mixer, manually whisk the flour, salt, sugar, yeast, and vital wheat gluten. Using your fingers, work the shortening into the dry ingredients until it breaks into pea-size pieces. Add 2¼ cups (540 ml) water and lock the bowl into the base of the mixer fitted with a dough hook. Mix on low speed until a shaggy dough ball forms, about 1 minute. Turn off the mixer and let the dough rest for 5 minutes (this will help the water properly hydrate the flour). Turn the mixer to medium-low speed and mix until the dough wraps itself around the dough hook and no chunks of flour remain, about 3 minutes. If the dough is crumbly and dry, add more water, 1 tablespoon at a time, until it just comes together. If the dough seems too wet, add more flour, 1 tablespoon at a time, until it just comes together.

Remove the bowl from the mixer, cover with a kitchen towel, and set aside for 1 hour.

Lightly flour your work surface and turn the dough out onto it. Using a knife or bench scraper, evenly divide the dough into 10 (4.5 oz/130 g) pieces. Drape the dough portions with a kitchen towel and let rest for 10 minutes. Uncover the dough and form each portion into a *boule* (a smooth ball) by shaping each piece into a rectangle and then gathering the corners of the dough into the center to form a bundle. Turn each bundle upside down so the seams are on the bottom. Cup the ball of dough with your hands and roll in tight circles on your work surface to create a tight seam on the bottom and a tense, smooth surface on top. Once you've formed all 10 *boules*, cover again with the kitchen towel and let them rest for 30 minutes.

Uncover the dough and shape each *boule* into a 6-inch (15 cm) *bâtard* (a short baguette). Turn each *boule* upside down so the seam faces you. Flatten the dough slightly with your hands so it roughly resembles a rectangle. With a short side facing you, fold the top of the dough toward its center and press down, then pick up this larger end and fold it down toward the bottom of the rectangle. You should have a thick log with one single seam at the bottom. Give the log a few rolls so it forms a tight cylinder 6 inches (15 cm) long. Apply a little extra pressure at the ends so they're slightly tapered. Transfer the loaves to a sheet pan or, preferably, a baguette pan (a perforated metal pan with indentations that helps baguettes brown and take shape), seam side down. Cover the loaves with a kitchen towel and and let the rolls rest, in the warmest spot in your kitchen, until they double in size and are puffy, about 3 hours.

Preheat the oven to 450°F (230°C/Gas Mark 8). About 5 minutes before you put the bread in the oven, set a baking dish with 6 ice cubes on the bottom rack of the oven (these will create steam when you bake the bread, preventing the crust from getting too hard).

Uncover the bread. Using a bread lame (or a very sharp paring knife or a serrated knife), make one long ¼ inch (.5 cm) deep slash down the length of each roll. Place the bread on the pan in the oven on the and add 6 more ice cubes to the baking dish.

Bake the bread, rotating the tray halfway through so the loaves brown evenly, until golden brown, 13 to 15 minutes.

Transfer the loaves to a wire rack to cool completely before eating. Leftovers can be stored in an airtight bag at room temperature and toasted before serving or warmed in a 300°F (150°C/Gas Mark 2) oven.

Brioche: Loaves, Rolls, and Ginger Sausage Rolls

**MAKES 2 LARGE LOAVES OR
22 INDIVIDUAL ROLLS**

8 eggs, divided
½ cup (120 ml) milk
1 teaspoon active dry yeast
4½ cups (540 g) bread (strong white) flour, plus extra for your work surface and your brioche molds (if using)
½ cup (100 g) sugar
1 tablespoon kosher (coarse) salt
¾ lb (345 g) cold butter, cut into small cubes
Baking spray
1 egg yolk

While developing the bakery side of Elizabeth Street Café, we knew we also needed excellent brioche, which is the key to our decadent Brioche French Toast with Blueberry Compote and Brown Butter Sauce (page 48). We also sometimes fold gingery pork sausage and scallions (spring onions) into the dough and bake individual rolls.

Crack 7 eggs into the bowl of a stand mixer and whisk to combine.

In a small pot set over low heat, warm the milk until it reaches (98°F/36°C).

Transfer the warm milk to cracked eggs and add the yeast, flour, sugar, and salt. Lock the bowl into the base of the mixer fitted with a paddle attachment and mix on low until the dough is just combined, about 1 minute. Increase the speed to medium-high and gradually add a couple butter cubes. Let the dough mix for about 15 seconds to let them incorporate and then add a couple more cubes. Repeat this process until all the butter is combined, and continue to mix the dough until it starts to pull away from the sides of the bowl, forms a ball on the paddle, and passes the windowpane test (see note on page 165), about 5 minutes.

Cover the bowl with plastic wrap (clingfilm) and let rest at room temperature for 1 hour. Refrigerate the dough in the bowl for at least 12 and up to 24 hours.

To form 2 loaves, divide the dough in half. Working with 1 piece at a time (keep the other piece covered) on a lightly floured work surface, flatten the dough slightly with your hands so that it roughly resembles a rectangle. With a short side facing you, fold the top of the dough toward its center and press down, then pick up this now larger end and fold it down toward the bottom of the rectangle. You should now have a thick log with one single seam at the bottom. Roll the log until it forms a tight cylinder, 9 inches (23 cm) long. Spray 2 (9 × 5-inch/23 × 12.5 cm) loaf pans with baking spray and transfer the loaves, seam side down.

To form individual rolls, working on a lightly floured work surface, divide the dough into 22 (2 oz/60 g) pieces. Shape each piece of dough into a rectangle, then gather the corners of the dough into the center to form a little bundle. Turn each bundle upside down so the seams are on the bottom and the smooth surface is on top. Cup the ball of dough with your hands and roll the dough in tight circles on your work surface to create a tight seam on the bottom and a tense, smooth surface on top.

Spray 22 brioche molds (or the wells of 2 standard muffin tins) with baking spray and lightly flour them. Transfer the *boules* to the molds, seam side down.

Cover the loaves or rolls, whichever you decided to make, with a kitchen towel and place in the warmest spot of your your home, away from any drafts. Let the brioche rest until doubled in size, about 2 hours.

Preheat the oven to 350°F (175°C/Gas Mark 4).

Beat the remaining egg together with the egg yolk. Uncover the rested brioche and brush with the egg wash. Bake until dark golden brown, about 45 minutes for the loaves or 20 minutes for the rolls. Let the brioche cool for 10 minutes before taking the brioche out of the pans or molds, then let the bread cool completely on a wire rack. Store leftovers in an airtight bag at room temperature and, before serving, toast or warm in a 300°F (150°C/Gas Mark 2) oven.

NOTE: To make Ginger Sausage Rolls, add 2 large handfuls of thinly sliced scallion (spring onion) greens to the dough right after it comes together but before adding the butter. Once the dough is mixed, fold in 1 recipe cooked and crumbled Ginger Sausage (see page 22). Follow the rest of the instructions for making individual rolls.

Classic Croissants

FOR THE POOLISH:

2¼ teaspoons active dry yeast

2½ cups (300 g) bread (strong white) flour

FOR THE CROISSANT DOUGH:

¾ cup plus 2 tablespoons (210 ml) milk

2¼ teaspoons active dry yeast

½ cup plus 3 tablespoons (140 g) sugar, divided

6 cups plus 2 tablespoons (735 g) bread (strong white) flour, plus extra as needed for your work surface

2 tablespoons kosher (coarse) salt

3 tablespoons (45 g) butter, plus extra for greasing the bowl

1 egg

1 egg yolk

FOR THE BEURRAGE:

1 lb (455 g) butter (preferably a European-style high-fat butter), at room temperature

Figuring out the perfect croissant recipe occupied our original pastry chef's time while we were opening Elizabeth Street Café. Making a poolish, a pre-fermented dough, is essential for croissants, since it adds great developed flavor and reliable leavening to the finished pastry. The carefully made dough gets folded with lots of butter (this layer is called the *beurrage*) and the final result is lofty, crispy croissants with tender, rich interiors.

The secret to making croissants at home lies in planning ahead. Croissants don't require much effort—just patience between short periods of work. We always serve these warm because it guarantees a crisp outer layer and a soft inside.

MAKE THE POOLISH:

In a large bowl, combine the yeast with 1¼ cups (300 ml) warm water (98°F/36°C). Let the mixture sit until the yeast is dissolved and the surface is foamy. There should be a few bubbles—indicating the yeast is working. if not, check the expiration date and the water temperature, and try again with new yeast and water if necessary), about 10 minutes. Add the flour and stir to combine. Cover the mixture loosely with a kitchen towel or plastic wrap (clingfilm) and let sit at room temperature until doubled in size, about 2 hours. You can let it sit for up to another 2 hours before proceeding. Reserve the poolish.

MAKE THE CROISSANT DOUGH:

In a small pot set over low heat or in a microwave, warm the milk until it reaches 98°F/36°C. Transfer the milk to the bowl of a stand mixer fitted with a dough hook and add the yeast and 1 tablespoon of the sugar. Let the mixture sit until the surface is foamy and there are a few bubbles, about 10 minutes. Add the remaining ½ cup plus 2 tablespoons (125 g) sugar, the flour, salt, butter, and the reserved poolish. Mix on medium-low speed until a smooth dough forms around the hook and no longer sticks to the bottom of the bowl, about 5 minutes. If the dough is crumbly and dry, add more water, 1 tablespoon at a time, until it just comes together. If, on the other hand, the dough seems to be wet, add more flour, 1 tablespoon at a time, until it just comes together.

Transfer the dough to a lightly floured work surface and shape it into a ball. Cup the ball of dough with your hands and roll in tight circles on your work surface to create a tight seam on the bottom and a tense, smooth surface on top.

Lightly grease a large clean bowl with butter and transfer the dough to it, smooth side up. Coat the surface of the dough with a light coating of butter, cover the bowl with plastic wrap, and refrigerate the dough for 1 hour to let the glutens relax and give you time to form the *beurrage*.

MAKE THE BEURRAGE:

Place the butter between 2 large pieces of parchment paper and use a rolling pin to form it into a 12 × 18-inch (30 × 46 cm) rectangle with a thickness of ¼ inch (6 mm). Transfer the butter, still sandwiched in the parchment, to the refrigerator and chill until firm, about 1 hour.

MAKE THE CROISSANTS:

Take both the croissant dough and the *beurrage* out of the refrigerator and let them sit at room temperature for 10 minutes. They should be at the same temperature and just pliable enough to roll out.

Transfer the dough to a lightly floured work surface and use a rolling pin to roll it into a 12 × 18- inch (30 × 46 cm) rectangle. Peel off 1 piece of the parchment of the *beurrage* and place the butter in the center of the dough so the short sides of the butter block are flush with the long sides of the dough rectangle. Peel off the second piece of parchment. Fold the sides of dough on top of the butter like you're folding an envelope, so the butter is completely covered with dough.

Turn the dough, butter inside, upside down so the seams are lying on the work surface. Roll it out gently until the rectangle is ¾ inch (2 cm) thick. Fold the dough into thirds (as if folding the pages of a pamphlet over each other) and roll out again until the rectangle is ¾ inch (2 cm) thick. Repeat the process once more.

Wrap the dough in parchment paper and transfer it to the refrigerator to chill for 1 hour. Take the dough out of the refrigerator and repeat the folding and rolling process twice more with 4 folds/roll-outs. Wrap the dough in plastic wrap and refrigerate the dough for at least 1, and up to 24 hours. If the dough threatens to burst out of the plastic at any point, simply unwrap it, do an extra fold (giving you extra layers and deflating the dough a bit), and then rewrap the dough.

Line 2 sheet pans with parchment paper and set aside.

Take the dough out of the refrigerator and transfer it to a lightly floured work surface. Roll it out into a 15 × 18-inch (38 × 46 cm) rectangle about ⅓ inch (8.5 mm) thick. If the dough resists and is difficult to roll, let it rest for a few minutes before proceeding. Trim ½ inch (1 cm) from each edge of the dough (discard the trimmings or bake them alongside the croissants) so that the layers are exposed. Use a sharp knife or a pizza wheel to cut the dough into 8 (5 × 8-inch/13 × 20 cm) rectangles and then cut each rectangle in half diagonally so you end up with 16 triangles.

Gently stretch the base of each triangle to make each triangle as symmetrical as possible. Use a knife to make a ¼-inch (6 mm) incision in the center of each triangle base. Loosely roll the base of each triangle toward its tapered end. Tuck the tail underneath your croissant. Transfer the formed croissants to the lined sheet pans, evenly spacing them so they have room to grow. Loosely cover the croissants with plastic wrap and set aside in the warmest spot of your kitchen, away from any drafts. Let the croissants rest until they're doubled in size, the defined layers are visible, and they jiggle slightly when the tray is jostled, about 2 hours.

Preheat the oven to 375°F (190°C/Gas Mark 5).

In a small bowl, beat together the egg and egg yolk. Uncover the croissants and brush them with the egg wash. Bake until the croissants are golden brown, about 20 minutes.

Eat warm or at room temperature. The croissants are best consumed on the day they are made, but you can store them in a sealed bag at room temperature for up to 3 days. Warm them before serving or use the leftovers for the Blueberry Croissant Bread Pudding with Blueberry Sauce (page 128).

Chocolate Croissants

MAKES 16

1 lb (455 g) dark chocolate, roughly
    chopped
½ cup (120 ml) heavy (whipping) cream
Classic Croissants dough (page 170),
    made up until the point of being cut
1 egg
1 egg yolk

Most chocolate croissants are made with hard sticks of chocolate (chocolate batons in bakers' speak). This means that when you bite into your croissant, the chocolate is so hard that it snaps. The chocolate in our croissants is actually thick chocolate ganache. Once baked, the chocolate is soft enough to yield to a bite, but stiff enough to remain separate from the dough. The result is the most decadent chocolate croissant.

Line a 12-inch (30 cm) skillet with plastic wrap (clingfilm) and set aside.

Place the chocolate in a large bowl. In a small saucepan set over medium heat, warm the heavy cream until the edges bubble, just a few minutes. Remove from the heat and pour the hot cream over the chocolate; let the mixture sit for about 30 seconds just to warm the chocolate. Stir the chocolate and the cream together until all the chocolate is melted and the ganache is smooth. Use a silicone spatula to spread the chocolate mixture evenly into the lined skillet. Let the ganache sit until it reaches room temperature, then refrigerate until cold and stiff, about 1 hour.

Line 2 sheet pans with parchment paper and set aside.

Invert the ganache onto a cutting (chopping) board, then peel off the plastic wrap. Cut the ganache into 16 even pieces.

Cut the dough into 8 rectangles and cut each rectangle in half to form 16 rectangles. Place a portion of chocolate at the base of each piece of croissant dough. Loosely roll the dough into a log. Transfer the formed croissant to the lined sheet pans, and repeat with the remaining ingredients. When placing croissants onto sheet pans, spacing them evenly so they have room to grow. Loosely cover the croissants with plastic wrap and set them aside in the warmest spot of your kitchen, away from any drafts. Let the croissants rest until they're doubled in size, the defined layers are visible, and the croissants jiggle slightly the tray is jostled, about 2 hours.

Preheat the oven to 375°F (190°C/Gas Mark 5).

In a small bowl, beat together the egg and egg yolk. Uncover the croissants and brush them with the egg wash. Bake until the croissants are golden brown, about 20 minutes.

Eat warm or at room temperature. The croissants are best consumed on the day they are made, but you can store them in a sealed bag at room temperature for up to 3 days. Warm the croissants before serving.

Everything-Bagel Croissants

MAKES 16

¼ cup (20 g) dried chopped onion

2 tablespoons dried minced garlic

2 tablespoons poppy seeds

2 packages (8 oz/225 g each) cream
cheese, cold

Classic Croissants dough (page 170), made
up until the point of being cut
into triangles

1 egg

We love "everything" bagels and figured the only thing better than one with a thick schmear of cream cheese would be to fill a croissant with cream cheese and the spices and flavors on top of an everything bagel.

Line 2 sheet pans with parchment paper and set aside.

In a small bowl, combine the dried onion, garlic, and poppy seeds and set aside.

Cut each block of cream cheese into 8 pieces. Place a portion of cream cheese at the base of each triangle of croissant dough. Gently roll the base of each triangle toward its tapered end. Tuck the tail under the croissant. Transfer the formed croissants to the lined sheet pans, evenly spacing them so that they have room to grow. Loosely cover the croissants with plastic wrap (clingfilm) and set them aside in the warmest spot of your kitchen, away from any drafts. Let the croissants rest until they're doubled in size, the defined layers are visible, and the croissants jiggle slightly when the tray is jostled, about 2 hours.

Preheat the oven to 375°F (190°C/Gas Mark 5).

Uncover the croissants and transfer the sheet pans to the oven and bake until the croissants are golden brown, about 20 minutes. In a small bowl, beat the egg. Let the croissants cool for 20 minutes, then brush with the egg wash and sprinkle liberally with the everything-bagel mixture. Return the croissants to the oven and bake just to cook the egg wash and lightly toast the everything-bagel mixture, about 2 minutes (keep an eye on them as the poppy seeds can burn easily).

Eat warm or at room temperature. The croissants are best consumed on the day that they are made, but you can store them in a sealed bag at room temperature for up to 3 days. Warm them before serving.

Ham and Cheese Croissants

MAKES 16

1 lb (455 g) thinly sliced high-quality
    French ham
1 lb (455 g) thinly sliced Gruyère cheese
    (use one on the softer side)
Classic Croissants dough (page 170),
    made up until the point of being cut
    into triangles
1 egg
1 egg yolk

When we started making these croissants, we kept them small since the ham and cheese are both so rich. Each time our bakers took a new batch out of the oven, Larry, wanting them to be showstoppers, would say, "These need to be bigger." Fast-forward to now, and these croissants each currently clock in at nearly a half pound (quarter of a kilo).

Line 2 sheet pans with parchment paper and set aside.

Divide the ham and cheese between each triangle of croissant dough. Loosely roll the base of each triangle toward its tapered end. Tuck the tail underneath your croissant. Transfer the formed croissants to the lined sheet pans, evenly spacing them so they have room to grow. Loosely cover the croissants with plastic wrap (clingfilm) and set them aside in the warmest spot of your kitchen, away from any drafts. Let the croissants rest until doubled in size, the defined layers are visible, and the croissants jiggle slightly when the tray is jostled, about 2 hours.

Preheat the oven to 375°F (190°C/Gas Mark 5).

In a small bowl, beat together the egg and egg yolk. Uncover the croissants and brush them with the egg wash. Bake until the croissants are golden brown, about 20 minutes.

Eat warm or at room temperature. The croissants are best consumed on the day that they are made, but you can store them in a sealed bag at room temperature for up to 3 days. Warm the croissants before serving.

Financiers

MAKES 8

6 tablespoons (90 g) cold butter, cubed

¼ cup (40 g) toasted almonds

¼ cup plus 3 tablespoons (90 g) sugar

¼ cup plus 1 tablespoon (40 g) all-purpose (plain) flour

2 egg whites

¼ teaspoon vanilla extract

¼ teaspoon kosher (coarse) salt

1 small handful sliced almonds (optional)

Financiers are said to have originated in a bakery in Paris near the financial district. To drum up more business, the baker came up with these golden, rectangular cookie cakes made of toasted almonds and browned butter to resemble gold bars, which he then gave to the French bankers. Not only did his bakery become successful, the recipe is now replicated all over the world in French-inspired bakeries—including ours. Sometimes giving away a free sample is the best investment you can make.

Preheat the oven to 350°F (175°C/Gas Mark 4).

Melt the butter in a small saucepan set over high heat and bring to a boil, swirling the pan now and then (but not stirring the butter), until the butter turns hazelnut brown. Keep a close eye as the butter goes from brown to burnt very fast. Immediately, and carefully, pour the butter into a small bowl and set it aside for at least 15 minutes to cool down (you can do this up to 2 hours ahead and leave it at room temperature). Be sure to leave any dark bits of burnt butter at the bottom of the saucepan (discard them).

Meanwhile, place the almonds, sugar, and flour in a food processor and grind until very fine.

Put the almond mixture into a large bowl and add the egg whites, vanilla, and salt. Stir until evenly combined. Add the butter, about 1 tablespoon at a time, making sure it is completely mixed after each addition (to keep the batter from breaking). If any burnt sediment from the butter made its way into the bottom of the butter bowl, discard.

Spoon the batter evenly among 8 (4 × 2-inch/10 × 8 cm) nonstick financier molds and top with sliced almonds, if using. Bake until golden brown, 16 to 18 minutes. Transfer the financiers, in their molds, to a wire rack. When they reach room temperature, unmold and serve. The financiers are best served on the day they are made, but leftovers can be stored in an airtight container at room temperature for 1 day.

Chocolate and Five-Spice Bouchons

MAKES 16

½ cup (60 g) all-purpose (plain) flour

¾ cup (85 g) unsweetened cocoa powder, plus extra for dusting

¾ teaspoon kosher (coarse) salt

1 teaspoon five-spice powder

2 eggs

1 cup (200 g) sugar

½ teaspoon vanilla extract

½ lb (225 g) butter, melted and cooled

4 oz (115 g) dark chocolate (62% cacao), roughly chopped

Cooking spray

When we first opened ESC, we didn't have a refrigerated case, so we developed recipes for baked goods that could sit out at room temperature. These *bouchons*, another one of our classic French pastries, were perfect then and are still a favorite and bestselling item. Essentially small cylindrical brownies—bouchon means "cork" in French—these are as decadent as they are adorable. Since chocolate and spice go well together, we add five-spice powder to the batter for a Vietnamese spin. If you don't have bouchon molds, you can use a brownie pan instead and cut into squares for serving.

Preheat the oven to 350°F (175°C/Gas Mark 4).

Sift together the flour, cocoa powder, salt, and five-spice powder into a large bowl and set aside.

Place the eggs and sugar in the bowl of a stand mixer fitted with a paddle attachment and mix on medium speed until ribbons form (or use a bowl and an electric handheld mixer). Mix in the vanilla. Decrease the mixer speed to low and add one-third of the dry ingredients and mix until combined. Add one-third of the melted butter and mix until combined. Continue alternating additions of the dry ingredients and butter until combined. Fold in the chopped chocolate.

Spray 16 (3 oz/90 ml) nonstick *bouchon* molds with baking spray and distribute the batter among the molds. (You can use 2 small spoons or a plastic bag with its corner snipped.)

Bake the *bouchons* until they slightly rise out of their molds and their centers feel just set (it's okay if they're not totally set), about 25 minutes. Look for the same slight rise and ever-so-set center if baking in a brownie pan, which will take about 40 minutes. Transfer the *bouchons*, in their molds, to a wire rack until they are cool enough to handle; then flip the molds over to release. Serve warm or at room temperature. Leftovers can be stored in an airtight container at room temperature for up to 2 days.

Caneles

MAKES 12

2 cups plus 2 tablespoons (250 g)
  powdered (icing) sugar
¾ cup plus 2 tablespoons (100 g)
  all-purpose (plain) flour
1 teaspoon kosher (coarse) salt
1 large egg
3 egg yolks
1 vanilla bean pod, split
2 cups (475 ml) milk
7 tablespoons (105 g) butter, divided
¼ cup (60 ml) rum
2 oz (60 g) beeswax, chopped

These French pastries originated in the Bordeaux wine country. The story goes that winemakers used to combine egg whites with young wine to pull out tannins and other impurities. The winemakers were left with better-quality wine and unused egg yolks, which they would often give to bakers. The bakers started making *caneles*, small custardy cakes with ridged, caramelized edges. Traditionally, they are baked in copper molds brushed with beeswax to prevent sticking and to impart a honeylike flavor. We add a bit of rum to our batter, so the *caneles* become almost like tiny rum cakes.

In a large bowl, whisk together the powdered sugar, flour, and salt and reserve.

Place the egg and egg yolks in a large bowl and whisk together.

Scrape the vanilla beans out from the pod and place the beans along with the scraped pod into a small pot. Add the milk and 3 tablespoons (45 g) butter and set the pot over medium heat. Warm the mixture until bubbles appear on the edges of the pot. While whisking constantly, slowly pour the milk mixture into the eggs. Discard the vanilla bean pod.

While whisking, slowly pour the warm milk and egg mixture into the flour mixture. Strain the batter through a fine-mesh sieve into a large bowl and whisk in the rum. Set the batter aside until it cools to room temperature.

Cover the batter and refrigerate for at least 8 and up to 24 hours.

Place the beeswax and the remaining 4 tablespoons (60 g) butter in a small pot set over medium-low heat and stir until both are melted. Divide the beeswax mixture among 12 copper *canele* molds and use a brush to make sure the mixture coats every nook and crevice. Turn the molds upside down on some paper towels for a minute to capture excess beeswax mixture (this will help avoid pools of beeswax in the final *caneles*). Transfer the molds to the freezer, right side up, for 45 minutes. Meanwhile, take the batter out of the refrigerator and bring it to room temperature.

Preheat the oven to 375°F (190°C/Gas Mark 5).

Remove the molds from the freezer and evenly space them apart on a sheet pan. Give the batter a very gentle stir to mix together (it tends to separate). Distribute the batter evenly among the molds, filling each one about three-quarters full.

Bake the *caneles*, rotating the tray halfway through the baking process, until golden brown, about 45 minutes. Remove the sheet pan from the oven and, using tongs, a kitchen towel, and a knife to loosen the edges, remove the *caneles* from the molds and return the *caneles* to the sheet pan, curved side up. Return the *caneles* to the oven and continue to bake until they're dark brown, about 25 minutes. Transfer to a wire rack.

Serve at room temperature. The *caneles* are best served on the day they are made, but leftovers can be stored in an airtight container at room temperature for 1 day.

DRINKS

Vietnamese Iced Coffee

MAKES ABOUT 8 CUPS (2 LITERS)

1 cup (120 g) ground chicory coffee
8 cups (2 liters) boiling water
1 (14 oz/397 g) can sweetened
    condensed milk
Crushed ice, for serving

We make Vietnamese iced coffee in single servings using traditional Vietnamese coffee filters called *cà phê phinm*, though we recommend making it in a big batch at home using a standard drip coffee machine or a French press. Like many Vietnamese coffee aficionados, we use chicory coffee from the legendary Café du Monde in New Orleans, Louisiana. History tells us that during the French Civil War, it became customary to add chicory, the root of the endive plant, to stretch out coffee, which had become scarce and expensive. The French introduced chicory coffee to Vietnam and also brought it with them to New Orleans, which, incidentally, was settled by the French and is currently home to a huge Vietnamese population.

Place half the coffee in the base of a French press and add the hot water. Stir together and let the mixture sit for 4½ minutes. Press the coffee and then pour it into a pitcher (jug). Repeat with the remaining coffee and water. Stir in the condensed milk and then transfer the mixture to the refrigerator for at least 2 hours and up to overnight. Fill 4 tall glasses with crushed ice, pour the coffee over the ice, and serve immediately.

NOTE: To make traditional hot Vietnamese coffee, the gear is just as important as the ingredients. For a single coffee, place a spoonful of condensed milk in the bottom of a glass tumbler, preferably a Picardie glass. Place a *cà phê phin* (a small coffee percolator) on top of the glass and fill with ground chicory coffee and hot water and let the hot water drip directly onto the condensed milk. Stir together and drink immediately.

Cold-Brew Iced Coffee

MAKES 6 CUPS (1½ LITERS)

½ lb (230 g) coarsely ground medium-
    bodied coffee beans

While we love Vietnamese coffee, its sweetness makes it more of a special-occasion drink. That's where cold-brew coffee comes in. Cold brew coffee is less acidic than its hot-brewed cousin, making it easier on the digestive system. The Toddy paper filter and nylon strainer we call for below are uniquely designed for cold-brew filtration, extracting all the natural and delicious flavors of coffee and tea and leaving behind the bitter acids and oils attached to their warm-brew counterparts. You can find these items in specialty shops and online. You can also just mix the ground coffee with the water and strain it through a coffee filter or cheesecloth-lined fine-mesh sieve.

Place the coffee into a Toddy paper filter and insert the paper filter and grounds into a nylon strainer. Loosely tie the bag closed with kitchen string. Put the nylon strainer and its contents into a large pitcher (jug) and add 4¼ cups (1 liter) cold water. Gently massage the bag to be sure the grounds are fully saturated with water and there are no air pockets. Cover the pitcher with plastic wrap (clingfilm) and allow the coffee to brew at room temperature for 20 to 24 hours. Remove the strainer from the mixture and discard the paper filter and the coffee grounds (the nylon strainer can be rinsed and air-dried for later use). Add 3¼ cups (750 ml) cold water to the concentrated cold-brew coffee and refrigerate until cold, at least 2 hours. Serve over ice.

Watermelon and Thai Basil Shrub

SERVES 6

2 cups (260 g) cubed watermelon

½ cup (100 g) sugar

1 bunch Thai basil, plus 6 extra sprigs for garnish

½ cup (120 ml) white wine vinegar

Sparkling water, to taste

We love to have refreshing nonalcoholic drinks on the menu so all guests have options. Shrubs are flavored vinegars that get diluted with sparkling water. Let the vinegar mixture sit for at least a week to fully mature before serving, so be sure to plan ahead.

Combine the watermelon and sugar in a large bowl and toss together. Place the basil in a small nonreative bowl and pour in the vinegar. Cover each bowl with plastic wrap (clingfilm) and refrigerate for at least 24 and up to 48 hours.

Position a fine-mesh sieve over a clean, nonreactive bowl and add the watermelon and all the juice accumulated in its bowl to the sieve. Strain the mixture, pushing down gently on the watermelon to extract all the juice (but don't push too hard—you want just the clear juice, not puréed watermelon). Discard the watermelon (or snack on it). Pour the basil-infused vinegar through the sieve, combining the watermelon juice with the vinegar. Discard the basil.

Cover the liquid mixture and refrigerate for 1 week to let the flavors fully develop.

To serve, fill 6 tall glasses with ice and divide the vinegar mixture among the glasses. Dilute each one with sparkling water to taste. Garnish each drink with a sprig of Thai basil and serve immediately.

Celery and Coriander Shrub

SERVES 6

¼ cup (20 g) coriander seeds, crushed

3 cups (400 g) roughly chopped celery

½ cup (100 g) sugar

½ cup (120 ml) cider vinegar

Sparkling water, to taste

Shaved celery, for garnish

This celery and coriander shrub is our version of a Dr. Brown's Cel-Ray soda. Popular in many of New York's great old Jewish delicatessens, Cel-Ray soda is the traditional (and perfect) accompaniment to salty, acidic foods like pastrami sandwiches and sour pickles. We figured it would go well with the strong, assertive flavors on our menu, too. The combination of celery with coriander seeds is a great pairing and a nice way to incorporate the ever-present cilantro on our menu.

Place the coriander seeds in a dry skillet over medium heat and cook, swirling the pan, until the coriander is fragrant, about 1 minute. Pour the seeds onto a plate and let them cool to room temperature.

Transfer the seeds to a blender with the celery and ½ cup (120 ml) water. Blend until completely smooth, then strain through a fine-mesh sieve into a large nonreactive container with a tight-fitting lid. Press down on the celery mixture to extract all the juice (discard the solids).

Add the sugar and vinegar to the container and cover. Shake the container to dissolve the sugar. Refrigerate the mixture for 1 week, shaking the container well once a day or every other day.

To serve, fill 6 tall glasses with ice and divide the vinegar mixture among the glasses. Dilute each one with sparkling water to taste. Garnish with shaved celery and serve immediately.

Salted Lemonade

SERVES 6

12 lemons, halved crosswise
½ cup (100 g) granulated sugar
½ cup (100 g) kosher (coarse) salt
5 oz (140 g) palm sugar
1½ cups (360 ml) sparkling water
Crushed ice, for serving

Chanh muöi, salted and pickled lemons or limes, are a staple in Vietnamese cuisine (*chanh* means "lime" or "lemon" and *muöi* means "salt"). The process, like North African preserved lemons, involves packing citrus fruits tightly in salt in glass containers and setting them in the sun to pickle. The liquid that comes off the citrus is fragrant and distinctive. With the addition of sugar and sparkling water, it makes for a refreshing salted beverage, particularly thirst-quenching on hot Austin days.

Squeeze the juice from the lemons into a small nonreactive container and transfer the juiced lemon halves to a large nonreactive bowl. Sprinkle the lemon halves with the granulated sugar and salt and toss to combine. Cover the bowl with plastic wrap (clingfilm) and refrigerate for 24 hours to let the lemons lightly pickle. Cover the juice and reserve it in the refrigerator, too.

Combine 2 cups (475 ml) tap water with the palm sugar in a small saucepan set over high heat. Bring the mixture to a boil, then immediately reduce the heat and simmer, stirring to break up and dissolve the palm sugar, until the sugar is completely dissolved, about 5 minutes. Let the syrup cool to room temperature.

Transfer the cooled syrup and the reserved pickled lemons to a large pitcher (jug) and muddle them using a wooden spoon or even a potato masher. Stir in the reserved lemon juice, another 1 cup (240 ml) tap water, and the sparkling water. Fill 6 tall glasses with crushed ice and divide the mixture among them. Serve immediately.

Đà Nẵng Margarita

SERVES 6

3 limes, halved crosswise
2 tablespoons sugar
2 tablespoons kosher (coarse) salt
6 tablespoons agave nectar, divided
1½ cups (360 ml) blanco tequila, divided
6 tablespoons fresh orange juice, divided
6 pinches of Aleppo pepper
1½ cups (360 ml) sparkling water
Sambal oelek chile paste, for garnish
Thai basil sprigs, for garnish
Chiles de árbol, for garnish (optional)

When Salted Lemonade (recipe above) just isn't quite strong enough, enter our house margarita, made with salted limes. Named for Đà Nẵng, one of Vietnam's largest cities, this refreshing cocktail captures the beach vibes of the ever-evolving port city. The salted limes add a new dimension to a familiar drink and presalt your margarita. At the restaurant we serve this margarita in a take-out container, but at home, just use a large tumbler.

Place the limes in a large nonreactive container or bowl and sprinkle with the sugar and salt and toss to combine. Cover the bowl with plastic wrap (clingfilm) and refrigerate for 24 hours to let the limes lightly pickle.

When ready to serve, make 1 drink at a time by placing 1 lime half in a cocktail shaker with 1 tablespoon of the agave nectar and muddle until most of the lime juice is extracted. Add ¼ cup (60 ml) tequila, 1 tablespoon orange juice, and a pinch of Aleppo pepper. Fill the shaker with ice, close, and shake vigorously for 20 seconds. Pour into a tall glass, lime and all, and top with ¼ cup (60 ml) sparkling water. Garnish with *sambal oelek*, Thai basil, and chiles, if using. Repeat the process with the remaining ingredients to make 5 more drinks. Serve immediately.

Shady Blonde Brunch Punch

SERVES 6

FOR THE SIMPLE SYRUP:
½ cup (100 g) sugar

FOR THE PUNCH:
1½ cups (360 ml) fresh grapefruit juice
¾ cup (180 ml) Lillet Blanc
¾ cup (180 ml) dry gin (optional)
Crushed ice, for serving
6 thyme sprigs, for serving
3 cups (720 ml) prosecco or other dry
   sparkling wine, for serving

At Elizabeth Street Café, half our seating is outside, so during the summer months we set up patio misters and serve icy cold beverages to help our guests cool down (these drinks also offer a refreshing counterpoint to all the spicy food). The Shady Blonde is by far our most popular punch—and a real crowd pleaser. The combination of sparkling wine, grapefruit, and Lillet makes this punch incredibly easy to drink, and the thyme adds a savory note to round out the flavors. You could add gin, which with its herbal, botanical notes would lend itself well to the Shady Blonde's flavors.

MAKE THE SIMPLE SYRUP:
In a small saucepan set over high heat, combine the sugar with ½ cup (120 ml) water and bring to a boil. Reduce the heat and simmer, stirring, until the sugar is dissolved, about 2 minutes. Pour the syrup into a pitcher (jug) and let it cool completely.

MAKE THE PUNCH:
Add the grapefruit juice, Lillet Blanc, and gin, if using, to the pitcher with the simple syrup and stir well to combine. Fill 6 tall glasses with crushed ice and place a thyme sprig in each glass. Evenly divide the grapefruit mixture among the glasses and top each one with some of the prosecco. Serve immediately.

Blackberry Spritzer

SERVES 1

2 tablespoons simple syrup (recipe above)
1 blackberry
Crushed ice, for serving
⅓ cup (70 ml) sparkling wine
2 dashes Scrappy's lavender bitters
3 tablespoons sparkling water

This gorgeous mix of fresh blackberry and sparkling wine is our spin on Kir Royale, an aperitif of champagne and crème de cassis (a liquor made from black currants). Light and not overly boozy, this spritzer is delicious and refreshing at lunchtime—or before dinner.

Place the simple syrup and the blackberry in a highball glass and muddle together. Fill with crushed ice and pour in the sparkling wine and bitters and stir together. Top with the sparkling water and serve immediately.

Seeds and Stems Party Punch

SERVES 6

3 cups (720 ml) sake (preferably Gekkeikan brand)

3 cups (400 g) cubed fresh pineapple

½ cup (100 g) superfine (caster) sugar

1½ cups (360 ml) sparkling water

2 tablespoons basil seeds

¾ cup (180 ml) cachaça

6 sprigs Thai basil, for garnish

A lovely tropical punch, Seeds and Stems is all about the aromatic, almost floral combination of basil and pineapple. It's also one of our stronger drinks with a healthy dose of cachaça, Brazil's answer to rum. If you can't find cachaça, use any spirit made from raw sugar cane, but avoid those made from molasses—like dark Jamaican rum.

Place the sake, pineapple, and sugar in a large pitcher (jug) and stir until the sugar is dissolved. Let the mixture sit at room temperature for 1 to 2 hours to let the pineapple infuse into the sake. Strain the mixture through a fine-mesh sieve into a clean pitcher (discard the pineapple or snack on it). Stir in the sparkling water, basil seeds, and cachaça. Fill 6 tall glasses with ice and evenly divide the mixture among them. Garnish each drink with a Thai basil sprig and serve immediately.

The Pink Lychee

SERVES 1

¼ cup (60 ml) Lillet Rose

2 tablespoons lychee juice (from a can of lychees)

⅓ cup (70 ml) sparkling wine

1 lemon twist, for garnish

1 canned lychee, for garnish

Lillet Rose is a French aperitif with delicate floral notes. Cut with sparkling wine and sweetened with lychee, it makes for an elegant crowd-pleaser of a drink. For sparkling wine, we recommend Crémant de Bourgogne (a French sparkling wine).

Pour the Lillet, lychee juice, and sparkling wine into a champagne flute. Gently stir together and garnish with the lemon twist and the lychee. Serve immediately.

Monaco

SERVES 1

Kosher (coarse) salt
1 lemon wedge
¼ cup (60 ml) Salted Lemonade (page 190)
   or store-bought lemonade
⅓ cup (70 ml) light beer (preferably
   Kronenbourg or another light pilsner)
1 Luxardo maraschino cherry, for garnish

Half lemonade, half beer, and topped with a cherry, a Monaco is the ideal easygoing drink and one of the best complements to spicy food. Luxardo maraschino cherries are worth seeking out—their intense cherry flavor easily surpasses other jarred cherries.

Place a thin layer of salt on a small plate. Rub half of the rim of a tall glass with the lemon and roll that half around in the salt to coat. Carefully fill the glass with ice, being careful not to brush off the salt. Then pour in the lemonade, followed by the beer. Put the cherry on top and serve immediately.

Velvet Ace Party Punch

SERVES 6

1½ cups (360 ml) Velvet Falernum
¾ cup (180 ml) Bonal Gentiane Quina
¾ cup (180 ml) Cocchi Vermouth di Torino
¾ cup (180 ml) rye or bourbon (optional)
¾ cup (180 ml) sparkling water
12 dashes Fee Brothers black walnut bitters
Crushed ice, for serving
12 Luxardo maraschino cherries, for garnish
6 star anise, for garnish

Most of our drinks match, or at least complement, the bright and refreshing feeling of our restaurant and our food. This punch is the dark, heavily spiced standout. If you like Manhattans and other strong brown drinks, this one is for you. It features three interesting ingredients: Velvet Falernum, a spiced, sweet syrup extremely popular in Caribbean drinks; Bonal Gentiane Quina, a fortified wine that is herbal and bitter and leans toward licorice; and Cocchi Vermouth di Torino, a complex-tasting, Moscato-based sweet vermouth. Combined with a bit of rye (or bourbon) for buzz and sparkling water for fizz, these ingredients make for a complex and memorable combination.

Place the Velvet Falernum, Bonal Gentiane Quina, Cocchi di Torino, and rye (if using), sparkling water, and bitters in a large pitcher (jug) and stir together. Fill 6 glasses with crushed ice and evenly divide the drink among them. Garnish each drink with 2 cherries and a star anise. Serve immediately.

Cilantro Mojito

1 cup (250 g) demerara sugar
1 bunch fresh cilantro (coriander)
1½ oz (45 ml) Cocchi Americano
1 oz (30 ml) fresh lime juice
1½ oz (45 ml) white rum (optional)
Crushed ice, for serving
15 dashes Angostura bitters

Mojitos are usually made with a generous batch of fresh mint, but our version instead relies on cilantro (coriander) since we always have loads of it in our kitchen and are always looking for new ways to feature it.

In a 2-cup (500 ml) glass jar (jug), combine the demerara sugar with 1 cup (240 ml) boiling water; stir until the sugar fully dissolves. While the simple syrup is still hot, add all but a handful of cilantro and let sit for 2 to 5 hours; then discard cilantro.

Pick the leaves of most of remaining cilantro (leave a few sprigs for garnish) and, in a tall glass, muddle the leaves with 1½ oz (45 ml) cilantro simple syrup. (If you do not have a muddler, use a clean wooden spoon.) Add the Cocchi Americano, lime juice, and rum (if using) and stir to combine. Add a generous amount of crushed ice to the glass and float the bitters on top of the ice. Garnish with a cilantro sprig and a few loose cilantro leaves and serve. (Cover and refrigerate the remaining simple syrup for up to 1 week.)

Rising Sun

⅓ cup (80 ml) fresh blood orange juice
⅓ cup (65 g) sugar
1 bunch cilantro (coriander)
3 cups (720 ml) chilled dry sake
3 tablespoons yuzu juice
¾ cup (180 ml) chilled blanco tequila
  (optional)
1 cup (240 ml) very cold sparkling water
1 blood orange, ends trimmed, sliced into
  6 rounds, for garnish

This punch is inspired by a Mexican Paloma cocktail, made with grapefruit juice, tequila, and sparkling water. In place of the grapefruit, we use a combination of blood orange and yuzu, a Japanese citrus that tastes like lime with the volume turned all the way up.

In a small saucepan set over high heat, combine the blood orange juice and sugar and bring to a boil. Let the syrup cook until reduced by half, about 5 minutes. Turn off the heat and cool the syrup to room temperature.

Fill 6 tall glasses with ice. Divide the sake evenly among the glasses. Gently divide the blood orange syrup among the glasses, by carefully pouring it down the interior side of each glass to create a layering effect. Evenly divide the yuzu, tequila, and sparkling water in each glass. Garnish each drink with a slice of blood orange and serve.

Coconut Milk Punch

SERVES 6

3 (2-inch/5 cm) cinnamon sticks

¾ cup (150 g) sugar

2¼ cups (540 ml) sake (preferably an
unfiltered, or "cloudy," variety)

1 cup (240 ml) well-shaken full-fat coconut
milk

1 cup (240 ml) orange bitters

¾ cup (180 ml) Jamaican rum or cognac
(optional)

Crushed ice, for serving

6 pinches of ground cinnamon, for garnish

1 blood orange, ends trimmed, sliced into
6 rounds

This is our version of a holiday milk punch. In place of heavy (whipping) cream, milk, and nutmeg, we use coconut milk, toasted cinnamon syrup, and orange bitters. Great to drink year-round, this punch pairs well with spicy Vietnamese food.

In a small pot over medium heat, toast the cinnamon sticks, stirring, until fragrant, about 5 minutes. Add the sugar and ¾ cup (180 ml) water and bring to a boil, stirring to dissolve the sugar. Turn off the heat and let the syrup cool to room temperature. Strain the syrup into a pitcher (jug) and add the sake, coconut milk, bitters, and rum (if using). Stir together.

Fill 6 tall glasses with crushed ice and divide the punch among them. Garnish each drink with a pinch of cinnamon and a slice of blood orange. Serve immediately.

PANTRY

ESC Fragrant Chile Oil

MAKES ABOUT 2 CUPS (475 ML)

2¼ cups (540 ml) canola (rapeseed) or vegetable oil

15 whole *chiles de árbol*

⅓ cup (40 g) *gochugaru* (Korean chile powder) or dried red chile flakes

5 garlic cloves, crushed

1 (3-inch/7.5 cm) fresh ginger, roughly chopped and crushed

1 whole star anise

All great Asian restaurants have their own variation of spicy chile oil. Ours leans toward Vietnam with the addition of ginger and star anise. We experimented with different ratios of chile to oil and various types of whole and ground chiles and landed on this recipe. An essential component of our Cold Beef Tendon with Fish Sauce-Pickled Peppers (page 62), our Spicy Lamb Dan Dan Noodles with Thai Chile and Mint (page 112), and our Ginger-Chile Oil Dumplings (page 94), this oil is also good on just about everything, especially swirled into a bowl of hot broth.

Place all the ingredients in a small pot and bring to a boil. Reduce the heat and simmer, stirring now and then, until the garlic floats, about 3 minutes. Turn off the heat and let the oil come to room temperature. Strain the oil through a fine-mesh sieve into a jar (jug), cover, and store in the refrigerator for up to 2 weeks. Note that the oil gets thicker when cold and holds the flavors even better than if stored at room temperature.

Peanut Sauce

MAKES ¾ CUP (180 ML)

¼ cup (75 g) smooth peanut butter

2 tablespoons well-shaken full-fat coconut milk

2 tablespoons fresh lime juice

2 teaspoons soy sauce

1 teaspoon sriracha

½ teaspoon toasted sesame oil

1½ teaspoons packed dark brown sugar

½ teaspoon kosher (coarse) salt

1 tablespoon finely chopped cilantro (coriander) leaves

Most peanut sauces are so thick, you may as well just eat straight peanut butter. Ours is on the thinner side and perfect for dipping our spring rolls. Feel free to up the sriracha if you like your sauce extra spicy. You can also drizzle this sauce over noodles or serve it with grilled (griddled) chicken or shrimp (prawn) satays for dipping or with grain bowls.

Place the peanut butter, coconut milk, lime juice, soy sauce, sriracha, sesame oil, brown sugar, and salt in a blender, add 2 tablespoons water, and purée until smooth. Transfer the sauce to a small bowl and stir in the cilantro. Serve immediately or store in an airtight container in the refrigerator for up to 5 days.

ESC XO Sauce

6 tablespoons (30 g) dried medium pink
    shrimp (prawns)

¼ cup (60 ml) canola (rapeseed) oil,
    divided

1 slice ham (½ oz/15 g), minced (any nice
    deli ham is fine)

1 tablespoon dried Thai chile flakes

1 tablespoon minced fresh ginger

2 garlic cloves, minced

½ Fresno chile or other fresh red chile,
    stemmed and minced

1 small shallot, minced

½ teaspoon sugar

1 tablespoon fish sauce

2 teaspoons distilled white vinegar

XO sauce, made with dried seafood, originated in Hong Kong. Because of the sauce's intensity, we serve it sparingly. It's great with steamed rice wrapped in lotus leaves (page 116) and on steamed oysters (page 96).

Place the shrimp in a small bowl and cover with warm water. Soak the shrimp until they're softened, about 10 minutes. Drain the shrimp (discard the soaking liquid) and transfer them to a food processor. Pulse until they're finely ground. Reserve the shrimp (and don't clean the food processor just yet).

Heat 2 tablespoons of the oil in a medium skillet, add the ham, and cook over medium heat, stirring, until the ham begins to brown and crisp, about 2 minutes. Add the chile flakes and cook until fragrant and the oil is vibrant red, about 30 seconds. Reduce the heat to low and add the ginger, garlic, Fresno chile, and shallot and cook, stirring, until the aromatics are softened, about 5 minutes. Add the reserved shrimp and the remaining 2 tablespoons oil and cook, stirring now and then, until the oil is frothy and the mixture is dark red and extremely fragrant, about 10 minutes. Add ½ cup (120 ml) water and cook, stirring now and then, until the liquid is reduced by half, about 5 minutes. Transfer the mixture to the food processor and pulse until relatively smooth and well combined. Transfer the mixture to a bowl and stir in the sugar, fish sauce, and vinegar. Serve immediately or store in an airtight container in the refrigerator for up to 3 weeks.

Nuoc Cham

MAKES 2 CUPS (475 ML)

½ cup (120 ml) fish sauce
¼ cup (60 ml) unseasoned rice vinegar
3 tablespoons sugar
½ small garlic clove, minced
1 Thai bird chile, thinly sliced
¼ cup (60 ml) fresh lime juice

Nuoc cham is to a Vietnamese kitchen what ketchup is to an American one—served with many dishes. The sauce benefits from sitting awhile before serving so the flavors develop.

Place the fish sauce, vinegar, sugar, garlic, and chile in a small heavy-bottomed pot set over high heat and bring to a boil. Reduce the heat and simmer for 5 minutes to dissolve the sugar and infuse all the flavors. Pour the sauce into a small bowl and let cool to room temperature. Whisk in the lime juice and 1 cup (240 ml) water. Serve immediately or store in an airtight container in the refrigerator for up to 1 week.

Vegan Nuoc Cham

MAKES 1 CUP (240 ML)

¼ cup (60 ml) Bragg Liquid Aminos
¼ cup (60 ml) unseasoned rice vinegar
2 tablespoons sugar
2 Thai bird chile, thinly sliced
¼ teaspoon minced fresh ginger
½ small garlic clove, minced
2 tablespoons fresh lime juice

We set out to perfect our version of Nuoc Cham (above) and to come up with an equally good vegan version. Enter Bragg Liquid Aminos, a liquid protein concentrate made from soybeans. Its depth of flavor makes a great substitution for fish sauce.

Place all the ingredients in a medium bowl, add ¼ cup (60 ml) water, and whisk until the sugar dissolves. Let the mixture sit at room temperature for an hour before serving. Store in an airtight container in the refrigerator for up to 1 week.

Sweet Chile Vinegar

MAKES ½ CUP (120 ML)

3 tablespoons unseasoned rice vinegar
2 tablespoons distilled white vinegar
2 tablespoons sugar
2 Thai bird chiles, thinly sliced
½ teaspoon kosher (coarse) salt

This sweet-and-spicy vinegar, which we serve with all our spring rolls, also works as a light dressing for a cabbage slaw or drizzled over something simple like grilled (griddled) fish or fried chicken.

Place all the ingredients in a small bowl, add 1 tablespoon of warm water, and whisk until the sugar dissolves. Serve immediately or store in an airtight container in the refrigerator for up to 1 week.

Fish Sauce Caramel

MAKES 1¼ CUPS (300 ML)

1 tablespoon fresh lemon juice
1½ cups (300 g) sugar
Pinch of cream of tartar
3 scallions (spring onions), ends trimmed, finely chopped
3 tablespoons fish sauce
1 tablespoon *sambal oelek* chile paste

The combination of caramelized sugar and fish sauce is popular throughout Vietnam and first came to our attention through the venerable Charles Phan, a widely admired chef and cookbook author. We use our fish sauce caramel to drizzle on the fried chicken that goes into our steamed buns (page 65) and on our Grilled Rib-Eye Fried Rice (page 108). It's also a great counterpoint to anything spicy and can be turned into a delicious dressing when combined with equal parts fresh lime juice or rice vinegar.

Place the lemon juice, sugar, and cream of tartar in a small heavy-bottomed pot, add ¼ cup (60 ml) water, and stir to combine. The mixture should look like wet sand.

Set the pot over high heat and bring the mixture to a rolling boil. Holding the handle of the pot, swirl it to completely dissolve the sugar (do not mix with a spoon). Reduce the heat to medium-low and continue to cook the caramel, swirling the pot now and then, until it turns light blond, about 10 minutes. (Don't step away while making caramel. Once the color starts to turn, the caramel moves from blond to burnt very quickly.) Add the scallions and continue to cook, swirling the pot to help the scallions mix into the caramel and to cook the raw onion flavor out, about 2 minutes. Add the fish sauce, return the heat to high, and bring the mixture back up to a boil. Immediately turn off the heat and let the caramel cool to room temperature.

Once the caramel reaches room temperature, stir in the *sambal oelek.* Serve immediately or store in an airtight container in the refrigerator for up to 1 week. If you refrigerate the caramel, bring it to room temperature and give it a good stir before using, as it gets really thick.

Clarified Butter

MAKES ABOUT 1½ CUPS (345 G)

1 lb (455 g) butter, cubed

Clarified butter, also known as ghee, is made by removing the solid milk proteins from butter, leaving a clear, golden liquid better suited for cooking at high heat. Plain butter, with its milk solids, has a low smoking point—the temperature at which the butter starts to burn—when heated. We use clarified butter all the time, especially for breakfast dishes.

Line a fine mesh sieve with a coffee filter or a double layer of cheesecloth and set it over a small bowl.

In a saucepan set over high heat, melt the butter, and cook, without stirring, until the white milk proteins float to the surface, about 4 minutes. Let the butter come to a boil, and once the milk proteins are foamy, reduce the heat to medium and continue to simmer the butter gently until the solids sink to the bottom of the saucepan and the simmering mellows. Pour the butter through the lined sieve into the bowl. Discard the the milk solids. Use immediately or cool the clarified butter to room temperature and refrigerate in an airtight container for up to 6 months.

Mayonnaise

MAKES 1 CUP (240 ML)

1 egg yolk
Kosher (coarse) salt and black pepper
2 tablespoons fresh lemon juice, divided
1 cup (240 ml) canola (rapeseed) or
    vegetable oil
1 garlic clove, minced

With the exception of certain pantry (storecupboard) staples like fish sauce, we like to make everything on our menu from scratch. The reward of homemade mayonnaise is well worth the effort.

In a large bowl, whisk together the egg yolk, a pinch of salt, and 1 tablespoon of the lemon juice. Pour the oil into a small pitcher (a liquid measuring cup [jug] works well) to make it easy to pour slowly. While whisking the egg yolk mixture vigorously, slowly add the oil, drop by drop, until the mixture starts to thicken. Continue to whisk, but start pouring the oil a little bit more quickly in a constant thin stream. Once all the oil is incorporated, whisk in the remaining 1 tablespoon lemon juice and the garlic, and season the mayonnaise to taste with pepper and additional salt if needed. Serve immediately or store in an airtight container in the refrigerator for up to 1 week.

Red Roasted Pork Belly

SERVES 4

¼ cup (60 ml) canola (rapeseed) or
    vegetable oil
2 tablespoons annatto seeds
1 lb (455 g) pork belly, skin removed and
    discarded, or cured slab bacon (streaky)
1 teaspoon sugar
1 teaspoon kosher (coarse) salt

Essentially our homemade bacon (streaky), we slice and crisp this roasted pork belly all morning to serve with dishes like Crispy Vermicelli Cakes with the Works (page 24). We also use it during lunch and dinner to add major flavor to dishes like our Green Jungle Curry Noodles (page 109) and as a memorable filling for Steamed Buns, Just the Buns (page 64). Our method for roasting it is based on *char siu* pork, the proto-typical Cantonese roast pork dish. We use annatto seeds for natural color and a bit of flavor. The fat that accumulates in the pan while the pork belly cooks is just as valuable as the meat itself—use it to make fried rice, enrich noodles, or roast potatoes.

Heat the oil in a small pot, add the annatto seeds, and cook over low heat, stirring once or twice, until the seeds are fragrant and sizzling and the oil is brick red, about 5 minutes. Strain the oil through a fine-mesh sieve into a bowl and discard the annatto seeds. Let the oil cool to room temperature.

Season the pork all over with the sugar and the salt. Put the pork in a large reseal-able plastic bag and pour in the annatto oil. Squeeze all the air out of the bag so the oil is completely covering the pork. Place the bag in the refrigerator and let marinate for at least 4 hours and up to overnight.

Preheat the oven to 350°F (175°C/Gas Mark 4). Line a sheet pan with foil and set a roasting rack or cookie wire rack over it. Put the pork, thick fat side up, on the rack and drizzle whatever oil remains in the bag over the pork (it's okay if it drips into the pan). Roast the pork until most of the fat is rendered and the meat is gorgeously browned and crisp on the outside and very tender within (test with a paring knife), about 1½ hours.

Remove the pork from the oven and let it rest at least 10 minutes before serving. Reserve the bright red fat in the sheet pan for another use.

If you plan to slice the pork belly thinly (whether for frying like bacon or adding to soups like Bún Bo Hue on page 38), let the meat rest until it is at room temperature or, better yet, wrap it and refrigerate for up to 2 days. It will be much easier to slice when cold.

Stovetop Jasmine Rice

SERVES 4

1½ cups (330 g) long-grain jasmine rice
½ teaspoon kosher (coarse) salt

This is our go-to method for making long-grain jasmine rice on the stove. By rinsing the rice thoroughly before cooking, using a precise water-to-rice ratio, and covering the pot as tightly as possible with the help of some aluminum foil, the rice comes out perfectly every time. For a bit more flavor, add a small piece of peeled ginger and one-half star anise to the water, and discard them before serving.

Put the rice in a fine-mesh sieve and rinse with cool water until the water runs clear.

Place 2 cups (475 ml) water and the salt in a medium saucepan set over high heat and bring to a boil. Add the rinsed rice and boil, uncovered, for 1½ minutes. Immediately cover the saucepan tightly with aluminum foil, followed by a lid, and continue to cook on high heat for 30 seconds. Reduce the heat to the lowest possible setting and cook the rice for 10 minutes. Turn off the heat and let the rice sit, covered and undisturbed, for 10 final minutes. Uncover the rice, fluff with a fork, and serve immediately.

Marinated Hon Shimeji Mushrooms

MAKES 1 CUP (240 ML)

3 tablespoons unseasoned rice vinegar
1½ teaspoons fish sauce
3 tablespoons extra-virgin olive oil
2 cups (120 g) fresh *hon shimeji* (beech)
   mushrooms, tough stems discarded
2 small garlic cloves, thinly sliced
Black pepper

These mushrooms are essential for the Glass Noodle and Seared Flank Steak Salad (page 60) and the Akaushi Carpaccio with Seared Shishito Peppers and Marinated Mushrooms (page 92). We always make them in big batches since they hold up well, so they inevitably end up in lots of other dishes, too. Fish sauce makes the marinade essentially a pickle brine, and this pickling method works well not only for mushrooms but also for any type of vegetable, such as sliced jalapeños or shaved carrots. If you can't find beech mushrooms, use halved small white (button) mushrooms or quartered shiitakes.

In a large bowl, whisk together the vinegar, fish sauce, and 2 tablespoons of the oil and reserve the marinade.

Heat the remaining 1 tablespoon oil in a large skillet and, when piping hot, add the mushrooms and garlic and season them aggressively with pepper. Cook the mushrooms over high heat, stirring so that they don't brown, just until they're warm, about 30 seconds. Transfer the mushrooms to the bowl with the reserved marinade. Immediately cover the bowl with plastic wrap (clingfilm) and let the mushrooms sit until they reach room temperature, about 30 minutes. They will release liquid as they cool and should be fully submerged once at room temperature. Transfer the mushrooms to an airtight container and refrigerate for at least 1 hour to cool completely before serving. Store in the refrigerator for up to 1 week.

Simple Shaved Cabbage Salad

SERVES 4

½ small green cabbage (14 oz/400 g),
    thinly sliced

2 large handfuls cilantro (coriander) leaves,
    roughly chopped

3 tablespoons extra-virgin olive oil

2 tablespoons fresh lime juice

2 teaspoons fish sauce

½ teaspoon kosher (coarse) salt

½ teaspoon black pepper

We make this simple, crunchy cabbage salad to go alongside Sticky Rice in Lotus Leaves with Grilled Pork, Shiitakes, and Chinese Sausage (page 116), to offset the rich filling. It's also the perfect side dish to go with just about any Vietnamese food. For an easy and delicious dinner, marinate a skirt or flank steak (or chicken thighs or tofu) with equal parts fish sauce, water, and sugar, and then char the meat over a hot grill. Let the meat rest, then thinly slice it and serve with a heap of this salad.

Place all the ingredients in a large bowl and use your hands to mix the ingredients together. Serve immediately.

Spicy Kohlrabi and Ginger Salad

SERVES 4

½ cup (70 g) peeled and julienned kohlrabi

½ cup (70 g) peeled and julienned green
    mango

¼ cup (35 g) thinly julienned fresh ginger

2 tablespoons finely chopped cilantro
    (coriander)

2 tablespoons finely chopped Thai basil

2 Thai bird chile, thinly sliced

1 Fresno or other fresh red chile, stemmed
    and thinly sliced

¼ cup (60 ml) extra-virgin olive oil

¼ cup (60 ml) Nuoc Cham (page 208)

We came up with this crunchy, spicy salad as an accompaniment for the Whole Steamed Fish with Black Vinegar, Ginger and Lime (page 122), but it goes well with just about anything, like the Simple Shaved Cabbage Salad (above). Topped with plain grilled (griddled) shrimp (prawns) or chicken, this makes for a delicious and healthy lunch.

Place all the ingredients into a large bowl and toss gently to combine. Serve immediately.

Spicy House Kimchee

MAKES ABOUT 4 CUPS (730 G)

¾ lb (340 g) napa cabbage (½ medium
   head), cut into 1-inch (2.5 cm) pieces

2 teaspoons kosher (coarse) salt, plus extra
   if needed

½ English cucumber, thinly sliced

1 small carrot, julienned

3 oz (85 g) daikon radish (½ medium
   radish), julienned

1 jalapeño, stemmed and thinly sliced

1 Fresno or other fresh red chile, stemmed
   and thinly sliced

¼ large white onion, thinly sliced

6 scallions (spring onions), ends trimmed,
   thinly sliced

1 garlic clove, minced

1 teaspoon minced fresh ginger

½ teaspoon fish sauce

2 teaspoons unseasoned rice vinegar

¼ teaspoon granulated sugar

1 tablespoon *sambal oelek* chile sauce

1 teaspoon toasted sesame oil

1 tablespoon *gochugaru* (Korean chile
   powder)

Making real-deal, true kimchee breaks a lot of Texas health code rules, since it relies on natural fermentation and can raise red flags with health inspectors. To get around this, we developed this recipe using a little vinegar to speed along the pickling process. *Gochugaru*, Korean chile powder, is essential here and worth tracking down to get the proper bright red color and earthy, almost fruity flavor. Kimchee is great tossed with hot or cold rice noodles. It can also be finely chopped and mixed with rice vinegar and canola (rapeseed) oil to make a pesto-like dressing for shredded kohlrabi and napa cabbage.

Place the cabbage in a large bowl and sprinkle with the salt. Use your hands to aggressively mix them together, thoroughly bruising the cabbage by squeezing it until it wilts. Let the cabbage sit at room temperature for 1 hour to draw out most of sits liquid. Place the cabbage in a colander and press down to squeeze out all the excess water from the cabbage.

   Return the cabbage to the bowl and add the remaining ingredients. Mix the ingredients together very well and let the kimchee sit for 30 minutes at room temperature. Season the kimchee to taste with salt, if needed, and transfer to an airtight container.

   Before eating, refrigerate the kimchee for at least 2 days and for up to 1 week. Shake the container or stir the kimchee 1 or 2 times a day. It will continue to ferment and develop flavor the longer it sits.

Vietnamese Meat Stock

MAKES ABOUT 3 QUARTS (3 LITERS)

4 lb (2 kg) beef, pork, or chicken bones, or
    a combination (see headnote for more
    information)
1 large yellow onion, halved
1 (8-inch/20 cm) piece fresh ginger
2 large carrots, roughly chopped
2 large pieces (approximately
    3 × 6 inches/7 × 15 cm each) dried kombu
2 tablespoons whole black peppercorns
2 whole star anise
2 (3-inch/8 cm) cinnamon sticks
4 whole cloves
1½ tablespoons kosher (coarse) salt
1½ tablespoons sugar
¼ cup (60 ml) fish sauce

Our stocks (broths) are, no pun intended, the backbone of so many of our dishes, especially our soups. We cook them slowly to develop incredible flavor. The type of beef or pork bones used are important, as the more collagen—which makes the stock rich—that is released into the broth, the better. Pork rib and shank bones are great, as are beef knuckle and neck bones. Avoid marrowbones, because they will make the stock greasy. You can also combine the beef and pork bones for an even richer flavor. If using chicken bones, opt for backbones and wings, because they have the most collagen and are the most affordable. You can also make this stock with just chicken bones if you'd like.

Evenly divide the bones between 2 large pots (each at least 8 quarts/7.5 liters), cover with cold water, and set over high heat. Bring to a boil and boil rapidly for about 10 minutes. Drain the bones and discard the liquid. Rinse the bones well with cold water and return them to the pots. Set the pots over high heat and cover the bones with 2½ quarts (2.3 liters) water and bring to a simmer. Regulate the heat to keep the liquid at a simmer, and skim the stock (broth) for the first 30 minutes of whatever scum rises to the top.

While the stock is simmering, using tongs, char the onion and ginger on all sides using the open flame of a stove (or under a hot broiler [grill] if you don't have a gas stove).

Once the stock has simmered for 30 minutes, add the charred onion and ginger, as well as the carrots, kombu, peppercorns, star anise, cinnamon, and cloves to the pots, evenly dividing the aromatics. Simmer the stock over very low heat for 8 hours, adding splashes of water as needed if the liquid reduces below the bones.

Pour the stock from both pots through a sieve into a large clean pot and skim off as much fat as possible. Whisk the salt, sugar, and fish sauce into the stock. Use immediately or cool the stock to room temperature and store in an airtight container in the refrigerator for up to 4 days (or freeze for up to 1 month).

Vietnamese Vegetarian Stock

MAKES 4 QUARTS (4 LITERS)

1 large white onion, unpeeled and roughly
 chopped
1 (3-inch/7.5 cm) piece fresh ginger,
 unpeeled and thinly sliced
6 scallions (spring onions), ends trimmed,
 cut into 2-inch (5 cm) pieces
6 carrots, unpeeled and roughly chopped
12 fresh white (button) mushrooms
12 fresh shiitake mushrooms, stems left
 intact
¼ medium napa cabbage, roughly chopped
4 whole cloves
1 (2-inch/5 cm) cinnamon stick
2 whole star anise
1 teaspoon whole black peppercorns
1 large piece (approximately 3 × 6 inches/
 7 × 15 cm) dried kombu
3 tablespoons sugar, plus extra to taste
3 tablespoons kosher (coarse) salt, plus
 extra to taste

This is an intensely flavored, quickly made stock (broth). Our meat stock at ESC takes awhile to prepare (extracting flavor from bones is a time-consuming process), but this mushroom-based version takes only a half hour. Essential for Spicy Vegetarian Pho (page 82), this stock can be used in place of any of our meat stocks to make dishes vegetarian.

Place the onion, ginger, scallions, carrots, mushrooms, cabbage, cloves, cinnamon, star anise, peppercorns, kombu, and 4 quarts (4 liters) water in a large pot set over high heat. Bring the mixture to a boil, then reduce the heat and simmer until the vegetables are very soft and the stock (broth) is fragrant, about 30 minutes. Pour the stock through a sieve into a clean pot set over low heat and discard the aromatics. Add the sugar and salt to the stock and whisk until they dissolve. Season the stock to taste with sugar and salt as needed. Use immediately or let cool to room temperature. Store the stock in an airtight container in the refrigerator for up to 4 days (or freeze for up to 1 month).

Notes on Pantry Ingredients and Equipment

SAUCES AND LIQUIDS

Bragg Liquid Aminos, a liquid protein concentrate derived from soybeans, is an excellent stand-in for fish sauce if you are vegetarian or vegan.

Canned coconut milk is not the liquid from inside of a coconut but rather the liquid that results when coconut meat is blended with water. It is rich, flavorful, and supremely creamy. We use it in cocktails and in many savory dishes. Chaokoh is our favorite brand.

Fish sauce, a condiment made from fermented anchovies, is used in many Vietnamese dishes. A little goes a long way, and its flavor is what makes so many dishes taste distinctly Southeast Asian. We prefer fish sauce brands with the fewest ingredients. Red Boat and Megachef are our favorites, since they contain just anchovy, water, and salt. We mostly use them for finishing dishes, much like using the highest-quality olive oil to dress your salads. Squid is also a good brand though has a little sugar.

Gochujang is a thick Korean chile paste made primarily of *gochugaru*, Korean red chile powder, mixed with glutinous rice flour, salt, and fermented soybeans. It is not as spicy as *sambal oelek* or sriracha. Wang is our favorite brand.

Hoisin sauce is basically Chinese barbecue sauce. Dark and thick, hoisin is made mostly with soybeans, chiles, garlic, sugar, and spices. We use Lee Kum Kee brand, but we find all hoisin sauce a little sweet and flat, so we always add a little rice vinegar and fresh lime juice to brighten it up.

Rice vinegar is, no surprise, vinegar made from fermented rice. It is light and almost neutral in taste. Marukan is the brand we use.

Sambal oelek chile paste is an Indonesian condiment made of red chile peppers and sometimes is flavored with garlic, shrimp (prawn) paste, or ginger. We use the one made by Huy Fong Foods that has a green top. *Sambal oelek* is great added to *bún* or *pho* for an extra salty, spicy kick.

Shrimp paste adds a major punch to Alehandro's Stir-Fried Rice Sticks with Steak, Crab, and Spicy Shrimp Paste (page 110) and is great in other noodle and stir-fry recipes. Our favorite brand is Por Kwan.

Soy sauce (also known as shoyu) is a dark, salty liquid made from a fermented paste of boiled soybeans. We use it in many dishes, as it is prevalent in many types of Asian cooking. Some versions are made with fermented grains, including wheat. Tamari, a Japanese soy sauce, usually contains little to no wheat—look for a gluten-free tamari if you have any issues consuming gluten. Yamasa is our favorite brand.

Sriracha is a spicy red pepper sauce made with chiles, vinegar, garlic, sugar, and salt. The brand we use is the one most common in the United States, made by Huy Fong Foods (with the rooster on the bottle).

Sweetened condensed milk is added to Vietnamese coffee and appears in many Vietnamese sweets. Longevity is our favorite brand.

Toasted sesame oil is strongly flavored and used more for seasoning than cooking, not only because it's so potent but also because it cannot withstand high heat. Kadoya is our favorite brand.

White shoyu is a soy sauce that is lighter, sweeter, and thinner than regular soy sauce. If you can't find it, use half as much regular soy sauce in its place. Morita is the most widely used brand in Japanese cuisine, and we love it for its clean, round flavor.

RICE, RICE PRODUCTS, AND NOODLES

Glass noodles are made from starchy ingredients like mung beans and sweet potatoes and go from opaque when dry to clear (hence the name glass) when cooked. We prefer those made from mung bean starch, and Chance Longkou Vermicelli, which come in a pink mesh bag, is our favorite brand. Bear in mind that glass noodles are hard to separate when dry, so if you don't plan on using the whole bag, try to find ones that come in portioned bunches.

Jasmine rice is fragrant, long-grain rice and its grains stay more separate than sticky rice.

Rice flour is available in nonglutinous white and brown varieties or a glutinous white variety. To achieve the right texture, we use both glutinous and nonglutinous rice flour to make our Crispy Pork and Shrimp Crêpe with Bean Sprouts (page 120) and Bánh Cuôn with Twice-Cooked Pork and Herb Salad (page 106). Erawan brand makes the rice flours we rely on.

Rice noodles are all made with the same ingredients—you are just choosing the size, shape, and texture. Look for Vietnamese brands and noodles made only with rice and water. Avoid other ingredients. Many rice noodles are labeled by size, indicating width (from small, or "S," the thinnest, to extra-large, or "XL," the widest). The noodles, thinner than "small," are vermicelli (known as *choa ching*). We get the best results from Wei-Chuan and Sailing Boat brands. For thicker noodles, look for *bún bo hue tuoi* on the package. For *pho*, we prefer fresh, semithick rice noodles, which tend to be softer and cook faster than dried ones. (Dried *pho* noodles also work well, they just need to cook longer. Also, look for noodles called rice sticks, medium-thick rice noodles (*bánh pho việt mien láo*). We use these in stir-fries.

Rice papers are thin, dry sheets made of rice flour that get pliable when dipped in water; they are essential for forming spring rolls. The square ones are easier to roll than the round ones since the corners help with folding. We prefer Bamboo Tree brand.

Thai sticky rice is short-grain, starch-rich rice that holds together well after steaming. It is also sometimes labeled sweet or glutinous rice.

Wheat and egg noodles are great substitutions for recipes using our house made noodles, like the Green Jungle Curry Noodles (page 109) and Spicy Lamb Dan Dan Noodles with Thai Chile and Mint (page 112). Fresh chow mein egg noodles and lo mein found in the refrigerated section in most Asian markets are pretty good. Wel-Pac dried lo mein (egg white only) is awesome and will work for these recipes and in countless stir-fries. For Chilled Dipping Noodles with Crab, Scallion, Bonito, and Black Vinegar (page 86), we use fresh Korean *udon jjajang* noodles and prefer the Assi brand.

OTHER DRY GOODS

Chiles de árbol are dried Mexican chiles, and while they might not be an obvious ingredient for a primarily Asian pantry (storecupboard), we rely on their heat for our ESC Fragrant Chile Oil (page 206) and in our the vinaigrette on our *Bánh Cuôn (*page 106).

Coconut jellies are used in our Vietnamese Coconut Sundae (page 150), and we like Jin Jin's lychee, mango, peach, and grape flavors, available on Amazon.com.

Cold Brew Iced Coffee (page 186) is one of our staples at ESC. We like Stumptown Hair Bender. For chicory coffee for Vietnamese Iced Coffee (page 186) and Vietnamese Coffee Pots de Crème (page 130), our preferred brand is Café du Monde from New Orleans.

Crispy fried shallots are a staple topping in Vietnamese dishes and we use store-bought ones, as do most Vietnamese restaurants. Fried garlic is also really good as a topping on curries and stir-fries and can be substituted for the triple-blanched garlic on our Steamed Oysters with Nuoc Cham, XO Sauce, and Crispy Garlic (page 96). For both shallots and garlic, Cock Brand Marque Deposee is the best.

Curry paste is a pre-mixed combination of aromatics and spices that greatly facilitates making curries by eliminating most of the preparation work. Mae Ploy is our favorite brand for both green and yellow curry.

Dried mushrooms, a big component of many of our dishes, are widely available at Asian grocery stores. The mushrooms we use the most are dried wood ear and white tree (or cloud) mushrooms. They don't have a lot of flavor and we use them for texture. Even when rehydrated, wood ear mushrooms retain their crunch.

Five-spice powder consists of ground star anise, cloves, cinnamon, pepper, and fennel. You could combine all those on your own, but we prefer the convenience of the mix. We use it in many dishes, including to flavor some of our sweets.

Fleur de sel (large-flaked sea salt) is great for finishing any dish when you want the briny crunch of salt. Maldon is our favorite brand.

Gochugaru, a primary ingredient in *gochujang* (page 221) is a coarse, mild Korean chile powder. We use it in many recipes such as our ESC Fragrant Chile Oil (page 206) and our green mango salad (page 68).

Kombu is a dried seaweed with a salty, briny flavor and is an essential component of all our stocks (broths).

Kosher (coarse) salt is our go-to salt, and Diamond Crystal is the brand we used to test the recipes in this book.

Madras curry powder refers to a specific combination of Indian spices used in curried dishes. We use it to flavor and color our Singapore Noodles with Gulf Shrimp and Roasted Pork (page 102), Crispy Pork and Shrimp Crêpe with Bean Sprouts (page 120), and in one of the variations of our *macarons* (page 154). Sun Brand, the kind that comes in a square tin, is our preferred brand.

Meringue powder is the "secret ingredient" in our *macarons*. Made of dried eggs whites, cornstarch (cornflour), and food gums, a little bit of it helps stabilize the meringue shells. It is available in the baking aisle of many grocery stores, in specialty baking stores, and online.

Palm sugar, a hard, light brown sugar that comes from drying the sugar palm sap (kind of like maple sugar), is a common sweetener in Vietnam. Because it comes in irregularly shaped pieces and is nearly impossible to gauge its quantity using a measuring spoon or cup, we recommend weighing it to get an accurate amount.

Pickled mustard greens are a staple of Chinese cooking and we use them to add a bit of funk to our Spicy Lamb Dan Dan Noodles with Thai Chile and Mint (page 112). Cock Brand Marque Deposee is the best.

Seto fumi furikake is a Japanese condiment made of flakes of dried seaweed, bonito (dried tuna), and sesame seeds. We sprinkle it on rice bowls, and it makes the simplest dishes like plain steamed rice and broccoli much tastier. JFC brand makes about eight excellent versions.

Small dried shrimp (prawns) are used in the same way that fish sauce is—a little goes a long way. Strong and assertive, the flavor of dried shrimp is unmistakable and a crucial component of our ESC XO Sauce (page 208) as well as our signature green mango salad (page 68).

PRODUCE AND OTHER FRESH INGREDIENTS

Coconut purée is necessary to make our Coconut-Lemongrass Sorbet (page 148), we use coconut purée and our preferred brand is Capfruit.

Fresh chiles and herbs are important to just about all our dishes. We go through so much of both that we planted a garden to keep up with our own demand. We favor Thai basil over standard basil since its anise flavor is so distinctive. Our favorite chile varieties are jalapeño, Fresno, Thai bird, serrano, and shishito. We never seed our chiles since we like the heat, but if you prefer your food more mild, feel free to remove the seeds before using.

Fresh ginger is essential to a Vietnamese pantry and we go through copious amounts of it at ESC. Always peel the ginger before using unless otherwise noted.

Fresh mushrooms feature prominently in many of our dishes, with our favorites including oyster, shiitake, and *hon shimeji* (also known as beech *bunashimeji*). These are all widely available in well-stocked grocery stores and in Asian grocery stores.

Kaffir lime leaves are packed with essential oils and have an intense flavor; they are also much easier to find than the limes themselves. You can find the leaves in many Asian grocery stores (sometimes in the freezer section) and online. If you can find a Kaffir lime tree, they do well potted in warm climates (and brought inside during freezes) and are really pretty. We love the flavor of the leaves in our Kaffir Lime Fried Chicken Steamed Buns (page 65) and Green Jungle Curry Noodles (page 109).

Wonton wrappers are one of the few things we purchase premade—some details are better left to the pros. They are essential for our Classic Tam Deli Wonton Soup (page 78) and Ginger–Chile Oil Dumplings (page 94). Golden Dragon is our favorite brand.

SPECIAL EQUIPMENT

For our Financiers (page 177), Bouchons (page 178), and Caneles (page 180), we use **metal molds** sold at kitchen supply stores. We prefer them to the more readily available silicone molds (they give the baked goods crispier edges). For *caneles*, our preference are the 2$\frac{3}{16}$-inch (5.5 cm) copper molds and for *bouchons*, we use the #4943 rum baba mold from Ateco that holds 3 fluid ounces (about 90 ml).

When we call for a **sheet pan**, we are referring to a sturdy stainless-steel rimmed 18×13-inch (46×33 cm) baking sheet. These are best purchased at a restaurant supply store and are often called half-sheet pans (because full-sheet pans, used often in commercial kitchens, are twice the size and don't fit in most standard home ovens).

We use a **steamer** for many items. A bamboo steamer works well at home in all instances except for our Steamed Buns, Just the Buns (page 64) since the bamboo colors them (which isn't the end of the world). If you're making these buns, seek out a stainless-steel steamer.

SOURCES FOR INGREDIENTS AND EQUIPMENT

Check out your local Asian markets for many of these ingredients and equipment and note that many fish stores have a good selection of Asian ingredients. For convenience, there are also many great deals found online.

Elizabeth Street Café Greatest Hits Playlist

When we opened ESC, we played a huge batch of songs delivered to the restaurant by Dom Wellhouse, aka DJ Lord Highpockets. Dom, our pal and husband of our opening pastry chef, Alexandra Manley, blended jams by French greats Serge Gainsbourg and Françoise Hardy with old Radio Thailand transmission clips and Cambodian psych rock. The music was rich with flavor. After a few months, the restaurant was so packed with guests all day that we needed more beats per minute, so we introduced electro-pop. Bands like the Chromatics, Chairlift, and Heavenly Beat had soft, pretty vocals over booming beats that fit the restaurant's juxtaposition of soft pastel walls and an extremely busy pace. This Sofia Coppola–soundtrack sound continues today with constant updates and a healthy dose of soul, funk, and R&B to keep folks moving.

Serge Gainsbourg—"L'anamour" (from *Jane Birkin/Serge Gainsbourg*)
Super-smooth vocals and string arrangements for a French cafe feel.

Ros Sereysothea—"Chnang Jas Bai Chgnainj" (from *Cambodian Rocks*)
Funky Radio Thailand transmission clips, including original radio VJ segments in between the songs … pretty funny!

Devendra Banhart—"Baby" (from *What Will We Be*)
Highlight from our breakfast playlist. Warm and fuzzy folk songs starting at 8 a.m.

Little Dragon—"Runabout" (from *Machine Dreams*)
First electronic band we played. Has a fun Japanese pop-song feel to it.

Chromatics—"The Page" (from *Kill for Love*)
Bubblegum rock with some crunchy guitar solos.

Chairlift—"Sidewalk Safari" (from *Something*)
Female vocals really work at ESC, so we kept looking for the prettiest vocals on fun, driving rhythms.

Heavenly Beat—"Honest" (from *Prominence*)
Slick electronic music incorporating worldly flute and string arrangements with breezy vocals.

Metronomy—"Do the Right Thing" (from *Not Made for Love*)
French-y pop.

Shintaro Sakamoto—"Mask on Mask" (from *How to Live with a Phantom*)
Japanese soul rocker. Smooth and funky sound to mix in with the electronic.

Charles Bradley—"You Put the Flame on It" (from *Victim of Love*)
Funk jam from this Baton Rouge soul singer.

Blood Orange—"Clipped" (from *Cupid Deluxe*)
When *Cupid Deluxe* album dropped, it perfectly fit our dinner atmosphere at ESC with its mix of electronic, r&b, and hip hop.

Knxwledge—"Trsh" (from *Hud Dreems*)
J Dilla-type instrumental tracks, which gives the playlists a bit more punch and attitude.

Flume featuring Jezzabell Doran—"Sleepless" (from *s/t*)
Incorporates the soul and hip-hop with the electro-pop we began with early on—all in one!

Neon Indian—"The Glitzy Hive" (from *VEGA INTL. Night School*)
ESC continues to be a very busy restaurant and songs like these are needed in each meal period to keep energy up!

Chance the Rapper featuring Knox Fortune—"All Night" (from *Coloring Book*)
Feel-good music.

Khruangbin—"People Everywhere (Still Alive)" (from *The Universe Smiles upon You*)
Local Texas soul band with elements of disco keeps us grooving.

Index

Acknowledgments

We would like to thank all our great customers who continue to make ESC the lively little place it is. You are the true regulars who let us know when everything's great, or even when something is a little off. Many of you are our investors and partners at ESC or at our other restaurants and this book could not have happened without y'all.

Thanks to Jon Williams for building the place with us, and for the continued improvements and friendship. Thanks to Jett and Foda Studio for all the great artwork and creativity throughout the years. To our buddy Evan Voyles for the iconic sign and always coming through, even if it's at the last minute. Arturo, thanks for being a great breakfast date and helping curate our little art collection.

Tons of love to all the cooks and bakers who have come and gone through our kitchens, especially Alex Manley and Jennifer Tucker for setting up the bakery and to Alejandro who has been with us since day one. We couldn't do any of this without our MMH team: Carla and Steve for supporting us and cooking the books; Ryan for designing some pretty uniforms, picking great tunes, and for all the help on this book. Thanks to all the hard working, friendly, and welcoming front-of-the-house, who have made ESC both a beloved neighborhood spot and a national destination. Special thanks to Will Hong for leading the team.

Thanks to the folks at Phaidon for giving us this opportunity, and to our team: photographer Evan Sung for being such a talented and friendly dude and our agent Angela Miller for talking us into writing a book. Special thanks to Julia Turshen for helping us choose our words and making our recipes more accessible.

Thanks to Larry's mom for introducing us to Tam Deli and turning us on to the great cuisine of Vietnam.

We hope this cookbook becomes a fish sauce-stained staple of your library. Thanks!

Tom & Larry

Recipe Notes

All herbs are fresh, unless otherwise specified.

All vegetables are medium size, unless otherwise specified.

Cream is 36–40% fat heavy (whipping) cream unless otherwise specified.

Eggs are large, unless otherwise specified.

Milk is whole at 3% fat, homogenized and lightly pasteurized, unless otherwise specified.

Yeast is instant, unless otherwise specified.

Salt is kosher (coarse) salt (Diamond Crystal), unless otherwise specified.

Cooking times are for guidance only, as individual ovens vary. If using a convection (fan) oven, follow the manufacturer's instructions concerning oven temperatures.

Exercise a high level of caution when following recipes involving any potentially hazardous activity, including the use of high temperatures, open flames, slaked lime, and when deep-frying. In particular, when deep-frying, add food carefully to avoid splashing, wear long sleeves, and never leave the pan unattended.

Some recipes include raw or very lightly cooked eggs, meat, or fish, and fermented products. These should be avoided by the elderly, infants, pregnant women, convalescents, and anyone with an impaired immune system.

Exercise caution when making fermented products, ensuring all equipment is spotlessly clean, and seek expert advice if in any doubt.

When no quantity is specified, for example of oils, salts, and herbs used for finishing dishes or for deep-frying, quantities are discretionary and flexible.

All herbs, shoots, flowers and leaves should be picked fresh from a clean source.

Both metric and imperial measures are used in this book. Follow one set of measurements throughout, not a mixture, as they are not interchangeable.

All spoon and cup measurements are level, unless otherwise stated. 1 teaspoon = 5 ml; 1 tablespoon = 15 ml.

Australian standard tablespoons are 20 ml, so Australian readers are advised to use 3 teaspoons in place of 1 tablespoon when measuring small quantities.

Phaidon Press Limited
Regent's Wharf
All Saints Street
London N1 9PA

Phaidon Press Inc.
65 Bleecker Street
New York, NY 10012

phaidon.com

First published 2017
© 2017 Phaidon Press Limited

ISBN (US edition) 978 0 7148 7395 4
ISBN (UK edition) 978 0 7148 7583 5

A CIP catalogue record for this book is
available from the British Library and
the Library of Congress.

Commissioning Editor: Emily Takoudes
Project Editor: Olga Massov
Production Controller: Nerissa Vales
Photography: Evan Sung
Cover Design: Julia Hasting
Design: Garrick Gott
Typesetting: Mónica Oliveira

Printed in China

The publisher would like to thank the
following individuals for their help:
Evelyn Battaglia, Molly Culver, Jude Grant, Kate
Slate, and Evan Sung.

Photograph on page 227 is by Molly Culver.